W9-BLC-477

Faith Goes to Work

Reflections from the Marketplace

Robert J. Banks

Wipf and Stock Publishers
EUGENE, OREGON

Wipf and Stock Publishers
199 West 8th Avenue, Suite 3
Eugene, Oregon 97401

Faith Goes to Work
By Banks, Robert J.
Copyright©1999 by Banks, Robert J.
ISBN: 1-57910-329-4
Publication date 8/16/1999

CONTENTS

Starting Points

Why a book on the relationship between faith and work for an audience chiefly made up of those whose lives are centered upon the church?

The reason is simple. By far the great majority of those who go to church are engaged in secular employment. These jobs, whether in the home, marketplace, or community, are the main context in which most believers work out their Christian obedience. Without help from their churches, many Christians will remain confused as to their proper responsibility in the workplace.

People are preoccupied with their work. The pressures they encounter there, the ethical dilemmas they face, the conflicts between job and family, and the threat of unemployment occupy a growing amount of their energy and time. For many people there is a greater reality and community in their place of work than in their church. Only a serious attempt by the churches to bridge the Sunday-Monday gap can alleviate this situation.

Churches are also concerned with reaching out to those who attend church intermittently or who do not attend church at all. These people are very open to Christians who will listen to their stories of the workplace. The majority of people also are open to hearing about ways in which their stories can be illumined by the Bible. As George Gallup Jr. has found, churches that reflect this attitude are attracting growing numbers of unchurched people.

Fortunately the connection between faith and work is drawing greater interest today from those engaged in teaching and writing about the Christian faith. There is a growing number of books on spirituality and the marketplace, some written out of personal experience, some more systematic in approach. Other books deal with the meaning and dilemmas of work and seek to bring a biblical perspective to bear upon them.

Though both types of books identify ways in which God is present in the workplace and attempt to explain how God is involved in what we do, they suffer from a common problem. In more scholarly writings, the connection between God and our work tends to be discussed in a way that is too general or abstract. More popular writings tend to be too simplistic and assume that quoting scripture verses, sometimes isolated from their context, is all that is required. Either way, the link between faith and work does not emerge as clearly as it might, and the real complexities of work are addressed inadequately.

This book aims to spell out more fully the connection between God's work and ours while recognizing the realities of contemporary work. We hope the book will be a resource for a broad audience: for pastors, Christian educators, and small group leaders in churches; for members of para-church organizations seeking to prepare Christians for their ministry in the marketplace; and for thoughtful lay people who either individually or in groups are looking for help in integrating their faith and their work.

Because work is so varied, it is impossible to do full justice to the range and diversity of work today within a single volume. To keep the book within manageable limits, we decided to restrict our focus to the public workplace, thereby omitting certain important areas of work such as the home and the community. This restriction should not be interpreted as a devaluation of what people do outside the so-called work force. This is not the view of the contributors to this volume.

The book focuses primarily on white-collar employment. Again this restriction is not meant in any way to devalue the contribution of blue-collar workers or those in more elite occupations. It is simply that a line had to be drawn, and that the world of middle class work is the one I know best. Perhaps this little volume will stimulate others to produce collections of other voices from the marketplace.

The contributors are united on the crucial importance of re-establishing the faith-work connection. Out of their reflection and experience they are convinced that

* Only so can Christians in the marketplace develop a holistic understanding of their faith rather than the compartmentalized one that tends to prevail.

* Only so can churches properly equip the people of God for their
   ministry in the world, their primary ministry, as well as in the
   church.

* Only so can society feel more powerfully the creative impact of
   Christian vision and values, commitment and compassion, that
   alone will overcome pressing and deep-seated problems.

All of the authors have had significant workplace experience or are
working with Christians in the workplace on a regular basis. Most of the
contributors are marketplace Christians and represent a broad range of
occupations. All of them have had some degree of seminary training or
have sought to educate themselves biblically and theologically. While
this in itself does not guarantee a greater capacity to link their faith and
their work, it does increase their potential to do so.

Our hope is that you will find this book useful in your circumstances, whether you are a pastor looking for ways of connecting your
preaching with the everyday world of your congregation, a Christian
educator seeking material to use in small group discussions, or a marketplace Christian wanting help in stimulating discussions among your
Christian colleagues on Christian responsibility in the workplace.

May you find the contributors efforts engaging, illuminating, and
challenging. May they stimulate you to support more energetically the
vital work of taking faith to work and developing a working faith that
will produce tangible changes in a needy world.

Robert Banks
Inauguration Day
January 1993

I.
The Sunday-Monday Gap: Resistances in Church and World to Connecting Faith and Work

Edward A. White

Introduction

Sixteen years ago, William Diehl asked:

> What has my church been *doing* to support my ministry in the various arenas of my life?
>   Very little.
>   I am now a sales manager for a major steel company. In the almost thirty years of my professional career, my church has never once suggested that there be any type of accounting of my on-the-job ministry to others. My church has never once offered to improve those skills which could make me a better minister, nor has it ever asked if I needed any kind of support in what I was doing. There has never been an inquiry into the types of ethical decisions I must face, or whether I seek to communicate the faith to my co-workers. I have never been in a congregation where there was any type of public affirmation of a ministry in my career. In short, I must conclude that my church really doesn't have the least interest in whether or how I minister in my daily work.[1]

How many of the people in our pews could make a similar statement?
    Thirty-five years ago a Dutch lay theologian named Hendrik Kraemer wrote a book entitled *A Theology of the Laity*.[2] In this book he described how the church had betrayed its original calling to be the people of God in the world. "Ministry," instead of being the work of the whole people of God and world centered, had become the work of a special class called "clergy" and was church-centered.

In the earliest church there were no clergy! Jesus was a lay person. The only ordination recorded in the Bible was baptism. The twelve disciples were lay persons. As was Paul. Ministry was the work of the whole people of God. Ministry was in the world and for the world. John 3:16 does not say "God so loved the church . . . ," it says "God so loved the world . . ."

It is the world that God is determined to redeem and all disciples are actors in the drama.

The church has gone astray, becoming an end in itself rather than a means to God's ends. Preoccupied with its own survival, the church has become an institution, largely owned and operated by a special class called clergy who are perceived to be *the* ministers.

Baptism has largely lost its meaning. In the early church, baptism represented the call to the full-time service of God. Now ordination has taken the place of baptism.

I once conducted a retreat for twenty-seven pastors. One of them mentioned that a friend of his had just "received the call to full-time Christian service." I asked what that meant.

"Oh," he said, "he got the call to go to seminary and become a preacher!"

I replied, "I thought we believed that every Christian was called to full-time Christian service. I thought that's what baptism meant . . . God's claim on our whole life . . . whether we're a homemaker, a school-teacher, or a lawyer."

"Oh well, that's true," he replied in a patronizing manner.

Irritated by his response I challenged the entire group: "How many of the members of your congregations really understand, believe, and practice the conviction that they have been called to full-time Christian service by virtue of their baptism?"

The previous speaker replied rather quickly; "Oh I suppose about ten percent."

I was stunned by the response of everyone else in the room. "No way!" they said. Half of them said "Maybe between one and two per-cent." The other half said, "Probably less than one percent."

If these congregations are typical of Protestant America, that means that ninety-nine percent of the Protestants in this country don't even know the meaning of their baptism. Why on earth would the good Lord want to increase our numbers? Can't you just picture Jesus saying to the original twelve: "Now I want one of you guys to follow me. The rest can go about your business as usual but join me occasionally for a Sunday morning service!"

Why doesn't the church take the vocation of its own members seriously? The answer, I believe, is because it is against the perceived self-interest of everyone concerned to do so! It is against the perceived self-interest of the clergy, the laity, the theological seminaries, the institutional church, and society at large.

Let us consider each of these constituencies.

The Clergy

Clergy are ordained to the "ministry of Word and Sacrament." By its very nature, this ministry is an act of faith. Most of the time the clergy are not really sure what difference this ministry makes. Occasionally a church member may tell them how a particular sermon affected them. But most of the time the laity are not aware of how the ministry of Word and Sacrament affects their lives. They internalize their experiences of worship and go on about their lives.

Most denominations require their congregations to compile an annual statistical report. The form does not normally ask whether lives are being transformed or people are discovering their call to ministry in daily life. The form asks "How many bucks, bodies, and buildings has your congregation generated this year?"

Pretty soon the preacher gets the message. What really counts in the church is not the ministry of Word and Sacrament, but the generation of positive statistics. The clergy are evaluated according to those numbers, and that is what they are rewarded for, usually with a call to a larger congregation with a bigger salary.

Caring about the quality and faithfulness of the lives of church members generally is not rewarded. Caring about the ministry in daily life of church members is not rewarded. What is rewarded is an increase in the number of pledging members. The model of *consumerism* replaces the model of *discipleship*. The church becomes the place where people go to have their religious needs met by the professional "need meeter," the clergyperson. If their needs are met, they join and are added to the church rolls.

Once these folks have joined, they become interesting to the clergy in terms of the ways they can contribute to the life of the institution. People are needed to help as church officers, Sunday school teachers, building and grounds superintendents, etc. The preacher recognizes and thanks those laity who provide service. Discipleship is understood primarily in terms of institutional activity.

Furthermore, many clergy have a need to be in control. Sometimes, if they try hard enough, they can be in control of the parish institution and what goes on there. However the weekday lives of parishioners in the world are beyond the control of the clergy. Indeed, most clergy are largely unfamiliar with the worlds in which their parishioners work. Years ago, in rural America, when the preacher visited the farmhouse, he was visiting both home and workplace. But in urban America, the workplace is separated from the home. Churches maintain some contact with the home, but precious little with the workplace.

Clergy are accustomed to being authorities on the subject of religion. In the world of the church they are relatively safe in exercising that authority. However, the workplace poses questions for which the clergy may have no ready answers. In fact, the clergy may not really understand the questions. Why allow one's vulnerabilities to be exposed? In the worlds of business, science, medicine, and law, the preacher may be seen as an uninformed lay person.

In addition, clergy are vulnerable to the whims of their congregations. The preacher is the leader but also an employee, answering to all of the members of the congregation. A significant number of clergy are involuntarily terminated each year. Hence it behooves them to confine themselves to meeting the traditional expectations of the membership and not go raising disturbing questions about the discipleship of these folks throughout the week. Job security is a powerful motivator.

Many clergy are already overextended trying to meet the seemingly limitless expectations of their congregations, leaving no time for visiting folks in the workplace.

Ministry in daily life can pose another problem for clergy. It can steal away their volunteers. Whatever happened to all those wonderful women who were the backbone of the church? Now they have jobs in the workplace. More than a few pastors feel forsaken.

Finally there is the issue of the peace and harmony of the congregation. The complex and troubling issues of the world and the workplace can be unsettling. We don't want any conflict around the church. As long as conversation sticks to the weather, the children, and the fortunes of professional football, there won't be any discomfort.

The Laity

There are a host of reasons why the laity tends to avoid the issue of ministry in daily life.

Accountability–Under the present formula, the laity go to church to have their religious needs met. In return they pay their pledges and provide some volunteer support. Discipleship is equated with church-related activities. There is something very manageable and comforting about this. We are only accountable to God for that part of our life that centers on church; the rest is ours to manage as we please. Ministry in daily life would require accountability to God and one another for our whole lives—in the home, community, and workplace, as well as in church. That might raise some sticky questions.

Success–We live in a culture that measures our worth by our accomplishments (justification by works). This is in direct conflict with the Gospel of justification by grace. We can handle the dichotomy if we can separate church life from the rest of life. As long as the two are separated, we will not experience conflict. Six days a week we can be driven by the compulsive need to climb the ladder of success. On the seventh day we can smile, shake hands, and sing hymns about "Amazing Grace."

Wealth and Comfort–Jesus had some harsh things to say about the rich, and He called the poor blessed. This is disquieting for those of us who enjoy a high standard of living (which we know the Gospel does not regard as high, not a standard, and not living). If we give generously to the church no one will ask what we do with the rest of our money.

Danger and Risk–We all know what happens to "whistle blowers." We may see things in the workplace that we know are wrong. However if we try to make things right, we face the prospect of rejection, isolation, and perhaps the loss of our job. We fear that if we try to stand up to the corporate powers of this world we will be bowled over like a feather in the wind.

Escape–We experience all kinds of ugliness out there in the world. Sometimes it seems as if what we call civilization is pretty much governed by the law of the jungle. At church we can get away from it all and find sanctuary and peace of mind. We don't want to be confronted with the very pain from which we are seeking relief.

Fear of Moralism–Our preacher doesn't understand our world. If she comes to visit us in the workplace we are likely to be subjected to a barrage of moralism and simplistic advice. Not helpful!

Low Self-Esteem–Ministry in daily life is a threatening idea. Ministry is exercised by people who have special God-given gifts. We don't have any special gifts. We work to keep bread on the table and that's enough. All this talk about the ministry of the laity reminds us of our inadequacy.

Compartmentalization–Clergy learn to speak theologicalese. Lawyers speak legalese. Government employees speak bureaucratese. Doctors speak medicalese. Each of us has our own area of expertise and we will all be most secure if we stay within our arena of competence. Of course this means that we can't have much meaningful dialogue, so the less said, the better.

Salvation–Because salvation is a private and personal matter and really has to do with life after death, it does not involve life in this world or our relationship to others. We come to church to have our conversation with our God in order to be reassured that we will have a place in the sun after it's all over.

Recognition–Our church asks us to stand up and be recognized and thanked for teaching in the Sunday school one hour a week. Our church never asks us to stand up and be recognized and thanked for teaching public school all week long. Now we know what really matters in the eyes of God.

Isolation–It can get pretty lonely out there in the world. Trying to express Christian values in a hostile culture is like swimming up Niagara Falls. Where can I find help and support in the effort to relate faith to daily life? Who can I trust enough to talk to? Who can I find who really understands my world? Who can I find who will really listen and not judge me?

The Institutional System of the Church

Institutional Survival—When church members are faithful in the workplace, it may help society and please God, but it doesn't help sustain the institutional church. It needs folks who will contribute money, time, and talent to the system. Let's be realistic. We are in competition with the world for the loyalty and energy of our members.

Competition—In this highly competitive society we are in competition with other denominations for members. If we get diverted from evangelizing and recruiting and invest energy in the issue of ministry in daily life, the other denominations will get all the new members. We have buildings, programs, and clergy to maintain. Like it or not, we have a bottom line, and that is money and people.

Conflict Avoidance—Conflict is bad for the church. It divides congregations and costs clergy their jobs. The complicated issues of the world and the workplace can only serve to generate more conflict. We already spend too much time trying to resolve existing conflicts.

Church Sponsored Programs—Churches sponsor a host of institutional programs that benefit a wide range of people from the cradle to the grave. If we lose our volunteers, these programs will go under.

The Seminaries

The theological seminaries are dedicated for the most part to providing an excellent academic preparation for clergy. In my experience the seminaries are successful in achieving that goal.

However, when I finished twenty-one years with National Capital Presbytery, I made a list of all the clergy who had left parishes unhappily during those years. There were ninety-one people on the list! Only one had to leave his congregation for what I would call intellectual or doctrinal reasons; he left to start his own independent church. In every other case, the reasons for the departure did not have to do with the intellect. They had to do with emotional and spiritual issues, such as:

"How secure am I in my sense of self? Does the competence or strength of others threaten me? Do I like being me? Do I project a shadow that inhibits the growth of those around me?"

"How clearly can I define myself? Can I state clearly where I stand

on controversial issues without being judgmental? Can I speak with
authority?"

"Do I see life as a battle ground? When in conflict do I seek a win/
win solution, or must others lose in order for me to win?"

"How clear am I about my possibilities and limitations? Does it feel
like the outcome of the struggle is all up to me? In the words of that
great prayer, do I 'have the courage to change what can be changed, the
serenity to accept what cannot be changed, and the wisdom to know the
one from the other'?"

"How grounded am I in the midst of ambiguity and conflict? Am I a
conflict avoider? When the pressure is on do I convey anxiety to others
or do I convey that 'inner peace which passes understanding,' thereby
encouraging others to be less fearful and more able to cope?"

"How ready am I to live into the pain in order to learn from it?"

"Have I come to terms with my fear of death? How do I feel about
taking risks that might result in personal rejection?"

"How liberated am I from the constraints of careerism and consumerism? Am I clear about the difference between the Gospel of grace and
the gospel of success or the gospel of personal self-fulfillment?"

By and large the seminaries do not concentrate on enabling people
to pursue these questions. The seminaries do a superb job of preparing
people's heads, but most clergy get in trouble because of underdeveloped
hearts and souls. These are essential to the task of empowering laity for
ministry in daily life!

The Society

Society doesn't want ministry in daily life one bit. Ministry in daily life
confronts the false values of careerism and consumerism on their own
turf. A society that believes in the gospel of self-fulfillment does not
want to hear the words of Paul: "Have this mind among you which you
have in Christ Jesus, who though He was in the form of God did not
count equality with God a thing to be grasped, but instead emptied himself taking the form of a servant . . ."[3]

A society devoted to the compulsive climbing of the ladder of
success does not want to hear about a Lord who lived a life of humble
service.

A society striving for a constantly expanding economy does not want to hear about stewardship.

Did you ever wonder what would happen if we could convince every citizen of the United States to be a good steward and make his or her present car last another year? We know they could do it because during World War II Americans had to: there were no new cars to buy.

But if Americans made their cars last another year, what would that do to the auto industry? What would it do to the steel industry? This society needs people to buy cars even if people don't need them. This society does not want to hear about stewardship!

This society wants a civil religion that will baptize and sanctify the *status quo*. The principalities and powers of this world do not want to hear about a transcendent God whose ways are not our ways.

Religion is OK as long as it remains within its own sphere. The church is useful as long as it minds its own business and helps to bind up the wounds of those victims of an unjust social order. But when Christians take their faith into the world there is likely to be trouble!

In her book *Do What You Love, The Money Will Follow*, Marsha Sinetar cites a national poll which concluded that, "ninety-five percent of America's working population does not enjoy the work they do."[4]

Ninety-five percent is hard for me to believe. That's nineteen out of every twenty people; I would have guessed seventy percent. I know a great many people who no longer find meaning in their job. It's just a way to keep bread on the table. If we believe that God has a purpose for each person's life, think what a missionary challenge it is to help all these bored and unhappy people to discover their purpose in life.

I believe the following facts are connected:

— Most of our institutions in this country are in a state of decline;
— Many of our people are unhappy and unfulfilled in their work; and
— The church does not take seriously God's call of its members to ministry in daily life.

It does seem as though ministry in daily life is not conducive to the perceived self-interest of everyone concerned. But there are grounds for hope.

Signs of Hope

It was Jesus who said "Whoever seeks their life will lose it, but whoever loses their life will preserve it."[5]

I think Jesus was referring to institutions as well as individuals!

Pain is a powerful teacher. As the institutional crises in our society continue to deepen, I experience an increased readiness to hear the message about ministry in daily life. As things grow worse, there is the possibility that people can become "sadder but wiser" and can listen with sensitized ears to hear a call from God.

What do we mean by call? We mean that God has a purpose for each person's life. The primary call is the call to discipleship. Jesus said to the first disciples, "Come and follow me."

The call is to *be* not merely to *do*. The *doing* becomes part of the living.

Baptism expresses God's claim on our life. Living the life of a disciple of Jesus is the fulfillment of our call from God in baptism.

Two Descriptions of a Disciple

The Book of Order of the Presbyterian Church U.S.A. describes the Christian life as follows:

"A faithful member accepts Christ's call to be involved responsibly in the ministry of His church. Such involvement includes:

a) proclaiming the Good News;

b) taking part in the common life and worship of a particular church;

c) praying and studying Scripture and the faith of the Christian Church;

d) supporting the work of the church through the giving of money, time, and talent;

e) participating in the governing responsibilities of the church;

f) demonstrating a new quality of life within and through the church;

g) responding to God's activity in the world through service to others;

h) living responsibly in the personal, family, vocational, political, cultural, and social relationships of life; and,

i) working in the world for peace, justice, freedom and human fulfillment."[6]

According to this sequence it takes the Presbyterians a long time to get out of the church and into the world. Nevertheless, these nine claims taken together constitute a comprehensive call to full-time Christian service.

The *Search Institute* has done a massive study of six major denominations, seeking to find out how effective these denominations were in developing mature disciples. A *mature disciple was defined as someone who:*

1. Trusts in God's saving grace and believes firmly in the humanity and divinity of Jesus.

2. Experiences a sense of personal well-being, security, and peace.

3. Integrates faith and life, seeing work, family, social relationships, and political choices as part of one's religious life.

4. Seeks spiritual growth through study, reflection, prayer, and discussion with others.

5. Seeks to be part of a community of believers in which people give witness to their faith and support and nourish one another.

6. Holds life affirming values, including commitment to racial and gender equality, affirmation of cultural and religious diversity, and a personal sense of responsibility for the welfare of others.

7. Advocates social and global change to bring about greater social justice.

8. Serves humanity, consistently and passionately, through acts of love and justice.[7]

These eight dimensions can be collapsed into two overall themes. A person of mature faith experiences both a life transforming relationship to a loving God—the vertical theme—and a consistent devotion to serving others—a horizontal theme. These themes capture the essence of ministry in daily life, seeing all of life as a response to the loving claim of God. *God has a purpose for each of us.*

In 1987, William Diehl wrote a book entitled *In Search Of Faithfulness.* He asked the question, "What are the marks of a *faithful* Christian executive in the business world?"

He solicited information from 174 top executives from his own Lutheran denomination. From their responses, he identified seven marks of faithfulness which these executives reflected to varying degrees:

1. A commitment to their own personal growth, including serious Bible study.

2. An active prayer life.

3. A commitment to participation in Christian community in the form of their congregation and in some cases also a Christian support group.

4. Stewardship in both the narrow and the broad sense: stewardship of one's wallet and stewardship of creation.

5. A commitment to justice.

6. A commitment to a simple life style.

7. A sense of call.

Bill asked each of these executives, "Do you feel called by God to your present occupation?" Nearly 31 percent answered yes, 34 percent answered no, and 35 percent weren't sure.[8]

Those who did have a sense of call scored visibly higher on all the other marks of faithfulness as if having that sense of call shaped their whole response to the claims of discipleship!

Here are some of Diehl's findings.

Of all the executives, 25.9 percent said that they read the Bible regularly. Among those who felt a strong sense of call, 72.7 percent read the Bible regularly.[9] Only 38.2 percent of those without a sense of call prayed regularly. Roughly 76 percent of the respondents who felt a call to their occupation had regular daily prayer.[10]

A little over 31 percent of all the executives indicated that they tithed. Among those with a sense of call, 52 percent tithed.[11]

Concerning influences on ethical decision making: 40.7 percent of the executives felt that religious training was very important, as compared to 60 percent of those with a sense of call.[12]

Finally, Diehl found that executives with a sense of call had a greater expectation of finding joy and meaning in their work.

The Witness of Those Who Are Doing It

Ron Melvin is a committed Lutheran. He is also an accountant with the U.S. Public Health Service. Thirteen years ago Ron discovered a discrepancy. It had to do with a major social program entitled *The Health Professions and Nursing Student Loan Program*, initiated in 1964-65. The federal government has invested over half a billion dollars over the years in that program, intended to exist in perpetuity as the low-interest student loans are repaid and the money is granted for new loans. The object is to make available up to $2,500 per year to worthy candidates with financial need who are preparing for health care professions.

The contract signed by the universities and the U.S. government indicated that while the government-granted monies were waiting to be disbursed, the universities could invest the funds and the interest would be added to the pool of available scholarship money. Many universities overlooked this provision and simply returned the earnings into their general funds.

The problem was first discovered in a midwestern state thirteen years ago by some state auditors. Ron began to explore the issue and discovered that the misappropriations were widespread. In 1986, 1,400 letters were sent out to the delinquent universities. Since that time, Ron has had the painstaking task of working out a solution with the approximately 200 of the major universities that receive roughly eighty percent of the money in the program. The schools have been approached one at a time to negotiate the problem and recover the misappropriated money for the federal scholarship loan fund. Throughout this process Ron has encountered resistance from superiors who wanted just to ignore the entire problem and avoid conflict with the universities.

As of this writing, Ron has recovered thirteen million dollars which translates into 5,200 additional scholarship loans. Before he retires, Ron expects to have recovered a total of twenty million dollars!

I doubt that there is a single major Protestant denomination in the U.S.A. today that would be prepared to raise and contribute twenty million dollars to help needy students enter the health care professions. Yet this task has been accomplished by a single lay person who sees his work as his vocation instead of just a job! What would our government be like if all our public servants had this sense of call about their work? How can we produce this sense of vocation in all of our church members?[13]

Notes

1. William Diehl, *Christianity and Real Life* (Philadelphia: Fortress Press, 1976), v-vi.

2. Hendrik Kraemer, *A Theology of The Laity (Philadelphia:* Westminster Press, 1958).

3. Philippians 2:5-7a (RSV).

4. Marsha Sinetar, *Do What You Love, The Money Will Follow* (New York: Dell, 1987), 90.

5. Luke 17:33 (RSV)

6. Presbyterian *Book of Order*, G 5.0102

7. P. Benson and C. Eklin, *Effective Christian Education: A National Study of Protestant Congregations* (Search Institute, March 1990), 10.

8. William Diehl, *In Search Of Faithfulness: Lessons From The Christian Community* (Philadelphia: Fortress Press, 1987), 31.

9. Ibid, 38-39.

10. Ibid, 50.

11. Ibid, 80.

12. Ibid, 94.

13. From an article by Edward White, "This Call's For You," *Workbook on Christian Vocation* (Louisville: PCUSA, 1993).

Questions for Discussion

1. In your experience, what prevents the church from taking ministry in daily life seriously?

2. What is your understanding of baptism?

3. How can we change the culture of the church so that workplace ministry would be recognized and rewarded?

4. Where do faith and daily life connect for you?

5. What do you want from the church to support your ministry in daily life?

II.
The Place of Work in the Divine Economy: God as Vocational Director and Model

Robert Banks

Few Christians see their daily work as directly connected to the calling and purposes of God. Those who do see a relationship often have only a partial awareness of the way the two are linked. Only some people experience a dramatic call from God to take up a particular type of work. A minority perceive their work as central to the concerns of the kingdom of God. I want to argue, however, that more people are drawn by God into a specific form of work than are aware of it. Further, more work than we realize has a role in fulfilling God's purposes.

In what follows I explore the variety of ways in which God leads people into divinely endorsed work. Current understanding of the meaning of the *call* of God is inadequate. This issue must be viewed broadly and deeply. I also want to identify the multiple ways in which God's presence and human activity overlap. This commonality is far more extensive than is usually recognized, but to appreciate it we have to broaden our perspective on God's activities.

God as Vocational Director

For many people referring to God as "vocational director" will seem strange. Yet this is an appropriate way of describing one of God's primary concerns. In the past this aspect of God's work has been described as the *call* of God. While this description is satisfactory, it can be misleading. God's vocational direction is broader than this traditional approach suggests.

The idea of a *call* is derived from such passages as Isaiah's well-known vision of God's heavenly court. At this divine board meeting Isaiah overheard God ask: "Whom will we send and who will go for us?" to which Isaiah replied: "Here am I, send me!" (Is. 6.8). It is not difficult to think of other examples from the Bible where people were directly challenged by God in a similar way. Moses, Samuel, Jonah, and Jeremiah immediately come to mind. Then there are people like Paul, who describe themselves as "called to be an apostle." (Rom.1.1).

There are broader ways in which the word *call* is used in the New Testament. Most often call refers to the way all those who have heard the word of Christ are challenged by God to respond to the Gospel itself (1 Cor.7.20). But today many have drawn the conclusion that people have only been recruited in to the divine workforce if they have had a dramatic encounter with God. This may come through hearing a sermon or an address, reading the Bible or some other book, receiving counsel, or a prophetic word from some other person.

In some churches the idea of call is tempered by the conviction that those who have been called are being led by God. In that sense, the call is broadened to embrace the way circumstances begin to point that person in a particular direction. It includes the church's affirmation of the person's demonstrated qualities and gifts. In virtually all cases, this call is to a ministry in a church or para-church setting or in a Christian or missionary organization.

Given this interpretation of what a call involves, it is not surprising that most Christians conclude that they have not experienced anything of this nature. Even those who sense that they are in the place where God wants them to be rarely speak of receiving a call to their work. This partially explains why the majority of ordinary Christians feel they are second-rate citizens of the kingdom of God, overshadowed by those who devote themselves to ministry in, or on behalf of, the church.

Closer inspection of ways God draws people into vocations outside the church and of the divine value placed upon their work suggests a different approach. Return for a moment to the biblical examples. All were either prophets or prophetic religious leaders. What about people involved in other kinds of work used by God, in particular those working in the marketplace?

We meet several of these marketplace workers early on in the Old Testament, but they continue to appear throughout the biblical narratives. It is worth looking more closely at a few examples:

Two Builder-Craftsmen. Bezalel and Ohaliab were responsible for
the building of the Tabernacle. Their skill in metalwork, masonry, car-
pentry, and design is described as a gift of the Spirit. But these men are
not drawn into this work through a personal encounter with God. Their
names are given to Moses by God, but Moses is the one who recruits
them. No doubt their hearts were stirred to participate in the work, but
there is no direct prophetic call (Ex. 31.1-11; 35.30-36.2).

A Beauty Queen. Esther was a young Jewish woman who won a
royal beauty contest and became the king's wife. This turn of events was
completely beyond her control and involved a deliberate personal decision to hide her Jewish identity. Despite this, she was drawn into a
political struggle to save her people from genocide. This challenge does
not issue directly from God, but through her uncle Mordecai. Though
she prays for guidance on the matter there is no mention of any overt
divine response. But she becomes convinced that she has "come to the
kingdom for such a time as this" and begins a subtle round of diplomacy
to save her threatened kinfolk (Est. 3-8).

Four Senior Administrators. How did Daniel and his friends
come to hold significant administrative posts in the land of their exile?
They were chosen to be trained as public servants because of their physical bearing, social connections, intellectual aptitude, and general knowledge. In particular they demonstrated a God-given capacity for learning
languages, understanding literature, and interpreting dreams. Despite an
unwillingness to engage in certain religious practices and a consistent
adherence to their own religion, Daniel and his friends are finally promoted to top positions in the civil service (Dan. 1-6).

A Governor. Nehemiah was a minor official in the court of the
Persian king. Nehemiah had a deep concern for the welfare of Jerusalem
and of the people left behind there as a result of exile. He questions
some Jews coming from a visit to their homeland and then prays that
God would open up the opportunity for him to return there so he can
rebuild the city. While he receives no direct answer to his prayers, his
sincere grief at the fate of his country prompts the king to enquire what
troubles him. The king then permits Nehemiah to return to Judaea as
governor and rebuild the city (Neh. 1-2).

A Businesswoman. Tabitha (or Dorcas) lived in the city of Joppa
on the Mediterranean coast and was well-known for her skills in designing and making clothes. She was also renowned for assisting the poor

and being a generous benefactor. We have no idea how this socially eminent widow came to understand her vocation, although she is very similar to the ideal woman described in Proverbs 31. It is likely that she followed Paul's advice (1 Cor. 9:20 ff) that new converts should work out their calling in their present situation and position (Acts 10.32-43).

These examples clearly show that God draws people into their divine work in a variety of ways. In none of these cases is there a prophetic call. This does not mean that this work is inferior to that of the prophets; it is simply different. What is crucial is whether the persons have a clear sense that they are in the positions God desires. That sense can be present even without a dramatic or prophetic call. As our chief vocational director, God is not bound to only one way of guiding us. In fact, God shows great versatility in this matter.

William Diehl provides an interesting case study that is relevant to this question. In preparation for his book *In Search of Faithfulness,* Diehl surveyed almost 200 Christian CEOs around the country. His aim was to identify what made some of these people more effective and integrated Christians than others. He discovered that the decisive factor was the individual's sense of vocation. Those CEOs with a sense of vocation consistently scored higher on all the indices of Christian faithfulness, for example, prayer and meditation, involvement in the church, personal maturity, financial generosity, and seeking justice in the workplace.[1] However, like Diehl himself, these people did not possess any dramatic sense of God's call.

Because we tend to restrict our understanding of vocation as a divine intervention that is heralded by a prophetic message, most marketplace Christians conclude that God has not brought them to the place they now occupy. This affects both their understanding of the value of their work, and how it contributes to God's kingdom. In part this explains the frequent disjunction that is observed between people's faith and work. Clearer teaching and discussion on this in sermons, classes, and small groups, as well as through workshops, seminars, and conferences, would make a real difference.

God as Vocational Model

God not only gives direction to us as we seek our divine vocation, but
provides a model for our work. Because there is overlap between divine
and human work, connections can be identified. Only a limited amount
of attention has been given to this by theologians, preachers, or ordinary
Christians. Yet, as W. R. Forrester in his book *Christian Vocation:
Studies in Faith and Work* states:

> If we are to be able to redeem men [and women] in our age of tech-
> niques and depersonalizing machinery, we must be able to make real
> to them the great truths of Creation, Providence and Grace, as these
> are personalized in the doctrine of vocation.[2]

We focus first on the most familiar aspects of God's work before touching briefly on several others.

Redemptive Work. God's saving activity rightly has priority in
any discussion of divine work. Everything God does revolves around
this. What took place in and through Christ lies at the center of human
history and the material universe, reconciling "all things, whether in
heaven or in earth" (Col. 1.19-20). This is why we prize the work of
evangelists, apologists, and church founders. This aspect of God's work
is also reflected by ordinary Christians whenever they speak up for God,
talk about Christ, or help start a church. Unfortunately in some quarters
it is *only* when someone is engaged in these activities that they are regarded as doing God's work. The workplace is perceived as sort of a
farm-system for the "real work" of God, a place for evangelization, and a
source of financial support for full-time evangelists and church-founders.
    We should "always be prepared to give an answer to anyone who
asks" about our faith or way of life (1 Pet. 3.15). C. S. Lewis is a fine
example of a lay person who did this. Most of his fiction writings (all
written as a hobby) are apologetic or evangelistic in intent. But as part of
his university responsibilities he also wrote several scholarly books that
reflect his central Christian convictions. (These are beautifully crafted,
also reflecting God's way of working). In some cases people's ordinary
employment does possess a redemptive dimension. This is certainly true
of many who are counsellors or social workers, as well as others involved

in negotiating an end to hostilities, in mediating divorce cases and other disputes, and in resolving neighborhood or racial conflicts.

This happens in other areas. For example, there are also screen writers and producers who are committed to developing redemptive motifs in their scripts. This does not mean that they overtly preach the Gospel, but that in the story a moment of transformation occurs through a word or action embodying faith, love, or hope. This approach demonstrates that all kinds of ordinary work can contain an authentically redemptive component.

Creative Work. God's work began long before Christ came into the world to redeem it. In Genesis, God is the creator, "In the beginning God created the heavens and the earth" (Gen. 1.1). This aspect of God's work is a constant feature of the biblical writings. Mostly this refers to God's fashioning the physical and human world. But it is also a way of describing the novel and surprising ways God shapes historical and future events. Divine dealings are always fresh, surprising, and a little paradoxical. Anything God puts a hand to is likely to have a creative edge. Creativity is integral to the divine character.

Though we are not able to create something completely out of nothing, we are able to imitate God in this respect. Our creative work is possible because God has planted within us the capacity to be creative. More emphatically, God continues to work in the world partly through human creative work. Some people engage in this without acknowledging that God is the source of their fresh inspiration. Others are fully conscious of God's role in their efforts. We are accustomed to thinking that some occupations are more creative than others. Certainly the arts do give the creative imagination considerable room for play. Musicians, painters, sculptors, writers, and film makers do reflect God's inventive approach to work. There is an obvious and direct connection between the two.

But creativity is broader than this. The whole range of crafts comes immediately to mind. The biblical writings often depict God as a craftsperson at work, for example, as a potter, metalworker, weaver, knitter, stonemason, carpenter, builder, or architect. In their own ways these occupations, as well as others ranging from gardening and landscape artistry, to interior design and urban planning, can be earthly manifestations of heavenly work. But any occupation or activity that has a touch of originality about it reflects something of God's creative work. In some fields there may be little room for this creativity, but rarely is the capacity for it altogether absent. Even routine activities are open to the play of the creative spirit and do not always need to be predictable or monotonous. Many homemakers, office workers, and factory hands have found ways of gracing aspects of their work with a creative touch. Their doing so is a testimony not only to the human, but also to the divine spirit at work.

Providential Work. Between God's creative and redemptive activity, as a kind of extension of the one and preparation of the other, is the vital bridge of God's providential work. The full range of what God brings, gives, and supplies to us is celebrated in many places in the Bible (Ps. 104). The connection between this and our work is frequently overlooked or minimized in Christian thinking, preaching, and teaching. Sometimes God's creative activity is spoken of in such a way as to encompass this. The work of divine providence includes all that God does to maintain the universe and human life in an orderly and beneficial fashion. This includes conserving, sustaining, and replenishing in addition to creating and redeeming the world. Basically it has to do with God being the daily provider of whatever is necessary to meet the material, animal, and human creation needs.

Many types of human work are similar in character. Bureaucracies make possible the smooth and efficient running of society. Public utility workers play a significant role in keeping the physical and social infrastructure going, as do entrepreneurs who build businesses and create jobs for others. Service occupations and trades exist to supply and support people, organizations, and institutions in a wide variety of ways, as well as to fix things that go wrong and remedy problems that arise. The lower-ranking civil servant or housing inspector, the trash collector and cab or bus driver, the garage mechanic or builder, all play their part here. At times these people help us out in ways that are especially providential. We literally "thank God" for them when they appear on the scene, or refer to them as "angels in disguise." Consciously or not, our language is appropriately theological here, and sometimes it is those with the humblest occupations who help us out most. Where, for example, would our multi-story office buildings be without janitors or cleaning services?

Most occupations contain an element of doing the groundwork, keeping the machinery going, or fixing what is broken. Even the most redemptive or creative work involves these practical elements. The evangelist has to plan as well as preach. The scriptwriter has to make deals as well as dream up stories. Housework and other chores are a significant part of homemaking. Maintenance and organization are integral to most forms of work. We should not chafe at this or regard such activity as inferior. Without it no significant work could be done. Perhaps the extraordinary patience of God stems in part from the amount of time and effort God continually puts into such work!

If there were time, we could look in detail at other aspects of God's work that have connections to the work we do. The brevity of the following references to these connections does not imply that they are less significant than the dimensions of divine activity already covered.

Justice Work. Though God's justice goes beyond giving people their fair and equal redress or due, and though human justice constantly fails to live up to this standard, there is a valid connection between the two. In some measure legislators and government regulators, judges and attorneys, supervisors, and para-legal workers play a role in the purposes of God in the world at large. It is not a slip on the part of Paul when he describes those who seek to reward good and punish evil as "servants (or ministers) of God" (Rom. 12.4). So, in a different way, are social activists, minority advocates, consumer protectors, and others. But in many types of work, including what takes place in the home, people apply equitable rules, seek to avoid discrimination, or adopt an affirmative action approach.

Compassionate Work. There is a distinct overlap between this dimension of God's work and justice work. Compare especially the divinely appointed "servant" described in the prophets (Is. 40-55). In linking God's activity here with its human counterpart, one thinks immediately of the helping professions, ranging from doctors, nurses and paramedics, psychologists, therapists, community workers, home visitors, personnel directors, and welfare agents. In addition to these, many people are involved in some kind of helping work in a part-time capacity or as part of their regular job responsibilities, both inside and outside the home.

Revelatory Work. Throughout the Bible, God is constantly described as the one who enlightens others about the truth. What was "hidden for long ages past" is now "revealed and made known . . . by the command of the eternal God" (Rom. 16.25-26). This is a fundamental dimension of God's work, without which we would not know anything about what God has done. While there are obvious and direct connections with the work of the preacher and teacher, echoes of the more general revealing, enlightening, educating activity of God occur in all work that seeks to bring truth and wisdom to others. Since, as has often been said, "all truth is God's truth," those who communicate truth of any kind, professors, teachers, writers, commentators, journalists, parents, humorists, or cartoonists, are to some degree engaged in divine work. Since helping others to learn wisdom is integral to many other activities, we should not limit this to occupations of an educational or informational kind.

Conclusion

The examples I have provided are not the only facets of God's work that can be correlated with human work. I have provided some key examples rather than cover the whole range of possibilities. Nor, in making these connections, am I overlooking the way so much human work obscures or perverts divine activity. Human work can easily turn into something that panders to people's acquisitive desires, becomes destructive rather than beneficial, or develops an idolatrous or demonic character. When this happens our work becomes the opposite of what God intended it to be. At the end of history God will "test the quality of each person's work" and all our "work will be shown for what it is" (1 Cor.3.13).

Even here, however, the Bible provides us with some useful categories for evaluating common attitudes about work. Fruitful correlations can be made between negative counterparts of God's approach to work and such erroneous attitudes towards human work. Let me give two brief illustrations of this.

The Bible condemns people who attempt to justify themselves by their own religious efforts rather than accept the fact that they have been justified by what Christ has done. Even where believers understand that they are justified by faith, in certain areas of their lives they may still tend to try and justify themselves. These days they are more likely to do this through their occupations rather than their church-related activities. For many people today their sense of self-worth, acceptance by others, and ultimate significance is tied up with their careers. This is true even for pastors and other church workers. But our worth, acceptance, and significance must not lie in our work, whether or not it allows us to influence or serve to the wider society. Otherwise those who are too young or too old to work, or those who are too physically or mentally challenged to work, have no value, can never find full acceptance, and have no wider contribution to make.

The Bible recounts many occasions on which the people of God turned their backs on God's commitment to them and gave themselves instead to other gods. In doing so they broke the terms of the covenant that God had established with them; they were not loyal to the mutual obligations of the covenant. These days it is the language of contract rather than covenant that pervades the world of work. Today's emphasis is on gaining the maximum advantage at the other's expense, making the agreement as easy to get out of as possible should need arise, even intending to break it should a better opportunity come along. In workplaces loyalty often is in small supply, both on the part of employer and employee. Unless we can reverse the tendency to turn all covenantal arrangements into weaker contractual ones, and to regard contractual promises and obligations as provisional and breakable, the whole world of work is likely to become even more jungle-like than it is now.

Apart from human work often tending to obscure or pervert God's approach to work, there is a further danger. Too often we succumb to the temptation to rate certain types of secular work as more closely reflecting divine concerns than others. So, for example, engaging in one of the "helping professions" is often regarded as more Christian than other kinds of work, such as banking, real estate, or running a company. This kind of distinction is merely a modern variant of the old dichotomy between monastic and ordinary work. The Reformers did away with such status distinctions, even with those between pastoral and lay work in their own churches. As Luther said:

> There is no work better than another to please God; to pour water, to wash dishes, to be a shoemaker, or an apostle, all are one, as touching the deed, to please God.3

Indeed one of our major weaknesses today is that there are too few Christians in occupations that are less overtly people-centered, especially in ones where there is the constant need for compromise or possibility of being compromised. Christians tend to gravitate to occupations that "pick up the pieces." If only more recognized the value of their vocation in the occupations that shape modern society, for example, finance, technology, politics, and mass media, they might help prevent everything falling apart for so many people. It is partly because Christians have too narrow a sense of call and cannot see the connection between such work and God's work that they take a detour in other directions.

Notes

1. William Diehl, *In Search of Faithfulness: Lessons From The Christian Community* (Philadelphia: Fortress, 1987), 198.
2. W .R. Forrester, *Christian Vocation: Studies in Faith and Work* (New York: Charles Scribner & Sons, 1953), 20.
3. Martin Luther, "Treatise on Good Works," J. Atkinson, ed. *Luther's Works*, Vol. 44, (Philadelphia: Fortress, 1966), 26-27.

Questions for Discussion

1. Have you been able to forge links between your faith and your work? Where did you find this help and how helpful was it?

2. To what extent are you conscious of a *call* or of the leading/guiding of God in connection with your work?

3. Can you think of other examples of marketplace believers in the Bible? What occupations do they represent and how did these figure in God's ongoing purposes for humankind?

4. What connections between your primary work and any facet of God's work can you discern?

Workplace Reflections

III.
High-Technology Work
and the New Creation:
Dealing with Intangibles, Ambiguities,
and Consequences

Hal Miller

Farmers are in touch with the soil and the cycle of birth and new life. Teachers transmit truths, old and new. Doctors cure, nurses heal, and storytellers pass on the wisdom of the past.

I work in the field of high-technology; it doesn't fall into any of these traditional groups. As a result, no one has really thought about its theological side. The traditional vocations of teaching, medicine, law, and the ministry have at least had some attention. Each has the advantage of dealing with the priceless—knowledge, health, justice, and eternal life—and so theologians and others have tried to think about what makes that work good work. High-technology work, my domain, deals with nothing so exalted. We spend our days building software to find and manipulate data or making control systems that do one very small and specific job like control a car's spark plugs. Worse, my work didn't even exist fifty years ago. If the theology of traditional work is spotty, the theology of high-technology work is nonexistent. Even though I'm writing these words with the result of high-technology work (a computer and word-processing software), the vocation that produced those products seems very strange from the viewpoint of traditional work. And the result is that, when I try to understand my work's place in the goals of the kingdom of God, I feel like I'm pretty much on my own. I can't look to the saints before me to see how they handled doing work like mine. They didn't.

Yet God is at work bringing new creation into the world. And high-technology work is that kind of stuff. People in my field take pride in the fact that we are on the cutting edge of the future. We are making tools and toys that people will consider commonplace a decade or so from now. We are working in the realm of innovation and dreams. Something about this work has a consonance with God's work, and that is worth exploring. In many ways, high-technology work is like other kinds of white collar work. When I'm at work I talk with co-workers, go to meetings, write memos, and do all the other things that many other people do. As a result, much of what I think of as the theology of high-technology work —how it relates to God's activity in the universe and my path following God—is the same as for a lawyer or production mana-ger. We all are faced with the complexities of human relationships, the pressures of deadlines, and the ambiguities of the business world.

And yet I also do things that, if I stop to think about them, are extraordinarily strange when compared to other professions. Ranked by the time spent talking, for example, my most significant conversation partner is a machine. I talk to it using a language I would never use with another person. People in other high-technology careers spend their days computing the trajectories of space ships or synthesizing DNA strands or designing chips and disk drives.

The world of a high-technology worker is a strange amalgam of the future and the past. We work on things that only a small percentage of the population understand in organizations that have all the problems and perplexities of any other organization. This strange combination gives high-technology work its particular complexion. While we work on the cutting edge, we face the same ancient issues of other workers. And, if the truth be told, most high-technology work is much like any other kind of work: repetitive and mundane. Computers, after all, are the stupidest sort of people; they always do what you say rather than what you mean.

In my experience, understanding the theology of work, that which makes it good from a Christian point of view, means wrestling with a set of problems. Much of the theology of high-technology work is common to any work. The meaning working gives, the divine directive to cultivate the creation, the importance of relating cooperatively with other people, all these things apply to all work. What makes high-technology work interesting theologically are the particular problems it poses. Resolving these problems is the beginning of a theology of high-technology work. The problems are fairly simple to state, but difficult to resolve. One summary might be that high-technology work:

— creates little that can be called a "product" in the normal sense;
— is often closely related to defense work; and,

— produces results that themselves create new problems for human societies.

If people are to try to live faithfully in high-technology jobs, they have to come to some tentative resolution of each of these problems. The resolution is, in each case, probably temporary, since each week at work seems to bring new challenges to the delicate balances we find in these complicated problems. But each is worth exploring for the insight it gives into the theology of high-technology work and its place amidst the vocations.

High-Technology Work and the Lack of a Product

Some people who work in high-technology jobs do create things people might recognize as products. These might be microprocessors or genetically engineered critters that eat oil spills or protect strawberries from freezing. Many of us, however, go home from work day after day with only an equation or a few lines of computer code to show for our efforts.

Trying to explain how my work is useful or satisfying is a real problem. Relatively few people understand it; you can imagine the problem I have telling my kids what I do all day.

I happen to make computer software, but other high-technology workers are in a similar situation. We make things you usually can't see, eat, or drive. Most of the time you can't even weigh them. What we make is quite literally insubstantial. There doesn't seem to be any *product* here at all.

Yet there was a time when doing a job that produced something so ethereal, so ephemeral, was considered the pinnacle of human work. The medieval doctors worked hard and long to produce their answers to how many angels could dance on the head of a pin. They thought that such work captured the essence of human existence. Any animal, after all, can provide food or shelter. Providing thoughts, though they are weightless, is what humans do best.

A thousand years ago, work like mine would have been considered a blessing. It would have been thought the most divine kind of work. Indeed, much high-technology work seems scarcely to touch the ground long enough for people to get a serious look at it. It is extremely detached from the commonplaces of life.

And yet it's not a different world at all. Cars and light bulbs, and even breakfast cereals, cannot be manufactured without the products produced by people like me. Although these products are anything but commonplace, they make the commonplaces of our life possible. In a sense, our creations are largely enabling: they do not serve as ends in themselves but as services that allow others to attain other ends.

There is here, I believe, something close to God's work in high-technology work. We who build the weightless and ephemeral are really at work providing the channels for others to create something more tangible. We provide the substrate on which others build, the lines through which they can communicate.

In some ways, high-technology work is much like God's own creation *ex nihilo*. Computer software starts with nothing and creates its own universe with a few lines of code. That universe might be a kids' alphabet-learning program or a spreadsheet, but the programmers build it from nothing. They tell the new creatures of their universe, the icons and mouse pointers and function keys, what they will do and how they will do it.

All this is almost never an end in itself. High-technology workers create so that others can create something else more substantial. We provide a service that allows others to provide something greater. We create products to give others the tools for creation. Very much like God who created a garden and set the first human there to tend and cultivate it, high-technology workers give others the tools and the context for *their* creativity.

High-Technology Work and Defense Work

Another of the basic problems of high-technology work for Christians is that so much of it seems to be defense or military work. Some of it, in this country, is done directly for the U. S. Department of Defense. Much of the rest relies for its health, either directly or indirectly, on military expenditures.

This relationship between high-technology work and the military is not particularly mysterious. Many of the demands for things on the cutting edge come from the military. Few others who buy products require that what they purchase be the most advanced possible.

So, if you work in the field, chances are you will do work, one way or another, for the military. This seems to create a problem for some Christians. In fact, it created a problem for me when I began working in high-technology. Even as a youngster, I wanted to do something meaningful as my work. I didn't really know what that might mean, so I thought of it in terms of helping other people or contributing to progress or other vague generalities.

When the opportunity to work in my current job presented itself, I had to stop and think about whether that life goal of doing something meaningful could include defense work. At the time, I didn't know. So I decided to take the job. My reasoning went like this. I had managed to live thirty-five years without finding out whether or not defense work could be meaningful. I had remained blissfully ignorant because I had kept my distance. By taking a job that had a defense-related component, I could give myself the opportunity to look at the problem firsthand. If it turned out that defense work violated my Christian vision of work, I could try to find another line of work. At least, then I would know.

In the years since I made that decision, I have come to realize that it was mostly my outsider's perspective on defense work that made it appear to be such a significant problem. At best, I didn't understand what was involved; at worst I thought other occupations were morally pure and those who did defense work were morally suspect. When you examine the problem from the inside, things look very different.

From the inside, defense work is another piece of the puzzle that is trying to live in a world touched by God but not yet healed. If God had not touched this world, the warmongers and conquistadors could rule unchallenged; if God had already healed the world, they would be banished. As it is, we live in an uncomfortable zone lying somewhere between the two. Defense work helps to maintain the balance.

This conclusion came, in part, from talking to those who were actually leaders in the military services and realizing that there were hardly any warmongers among them. They see war, as I do, as a failure. Sometimes it is necessary, but it always indicates that other, more humane efforts have failed. And the leaders in military services that I have met have a much more poignant sense than I of the terrible costs involved in that failure.

My current understanding of the problem of high-technology work and defense boils down to something like this. It is a tragic, regrettable

fact that the world is a dangerous place. I wish it were otherwise. I
believe that God will ultimately make it otherwise. But it is not otherwise now and will not be otherwise in the foreseeable future.

Peace may come to the Middle East, or it may not. Either outcome
changes little about the basic make-up of the world. For the foreseeable
future, the world will careen back and forth between peace and war, hope
and desperation. Peace will break out in Europe and war will consume
the Balkans. New world order or no new world order, our planet looks
like a drunken sailor staggering unpredictably this way or that.

And that staggering, more than anything else, makes the world a
dangerous place. The unpredictability of alliances and petty dictators
and national interests makes it important to face the danger in the world.
And, at best, that's what defense work is—facing up to the realities of a
dangerous place.

In this context defense work is not in itself bad. Nor is it good. It is
simply necessary. It is a tragic, regrettable result of the tragic, regrettable
fact that the world is a dangerous place. One thing it means to be redemptive in defense work (or in the military services, for that matter) is
to keep the sense that the whole enterprise is regrettable. If we who have
that sense abandon defense work as unclean, we leave it to those who
would envision conquest and war as noble and good. To avoid such a
world of warlords and conquerors, we who find it tragic need to populate
its ranks.

Much high-technology work that doesn't directly involve dealing
with the military is still defense work. I had a friend who worked for a
company that grew crystals, very large crystals. Measuring a yard or
more on the long axis, they had a number of commercial uses. But what
kept her company in business was slicing these crystals into thin panes
that were used to make the sighting windows for laser-guided bombs.

"When I started the job," she told me, "I was fascinated by the
technical problem of growing large crystals. I still am. It's very difficult, really. Controlling the cooling rate in the furnaces is always difficult and there are invariably outside factors to consider.

"But I had always thought of myself as a borderline pacifist. On
principle, I would never work for one of those big defense contractors.
And yet as I learned more about my job and our customers, I found out
that we were supplying the suppliers of big defense contractors with the
parts they needed to make their bombs."

Her problem is no different than that faced by many people working in high-technology professions: the initial applications for new or exotic technologies are quite often military. If you work in high-technology, you often work directly or indirectly to create systems that can be used to fight wars.

If you're interested in moralistic line-drawing, it's an interesting exercise. If you work for a defense contractor, then you are surely doing defense work. But if you work for a company that supplies parts to defense contractors are you doing defense work? What if you work for a company that supplies raw materials to a company that supplies parts to defense contractors? What if you work for a company that manages the health-care benefits plans for a defense contractor?

And so on. The modern economy is so closely interwoven that almost no one who works can work wholly untouched by defense work. Some pastors might be untouched. So might some publishers of children's books. But many of us make our living touching defense work one way or another. The line-drawing exercise, deciding which occupations are pure and which are tainted, is not the important one. Rather, the important activity is to keep alive the sense that any war, even a necessary one, is a failure.

If we can keep this perspective, defense work can be redeemed, even if it can never exactly be redemptive. People in defense work (and, by the way, almost never those who are *not* in defense work) can turn defense work in genuinely defensive directions, toward making the world a relatively safer place rather than a more fragile and brutal one.

The Results of High-Technology Work

A third problem in high-technology work is the double-edged nature of its results. High-technology work tends to create innovative things. As a result, we're unsure what uses are good and what are bad. By contrast, we have generations, sometimes centuries, of experience dealing with the products of traditional work. We know what the good and bad uses of traditional work are, and we can pretty easily tell the difference between the two.

Think, for example, of television. When it first became widely available in the 1950s, many parents saw it as an unprecedented boon in child care. I was among those mesmerized by *The Mickey Mouse Club*, *The Lone Ranger*, and *Sky King*. By the time I was eighteen, I was definitely an addict. Life without TV seemed unthinkable. Our lack of experience dealing with a medium as compelling as television left us unprepared for its dark side.

Parents are now a little better equipped to deal with their children's viewing habits, but this does not mean that we have mastered television. It is still a frighteningly effective advertising environment. It still retains its ability to make us believe what it portrays as truth. And it still projects the values and biases of the elites who control it. Only recently have the major networks realized, for example, that they overstep their bounds when they project winners of Presidential elections while people in California are still voting.

The high-technology workers who created the television and the systems that support it were no different from others who today work on analogous projects. Their work was technically engrossing, sometimes downright fun, and its results were interesting. Today, for example, medical researchers have found ways to use fetal tissue in therapies for some diseases. This is a boon to the people affected. And the work is surely engrossing. But, since the tissue in question ostensibly comes from aborted fetuses, we as a society are, even more profoundly than was the case with television, totally unprepared to face the moral problems these therapies create.

Today one of the significant areas of high-technology work is communication. People who work in my field are really doing two different tasks that help communication—enhancing it and broadening it. First, they are enhancing communication by making communication easier. When I graduated from high school, the quickest way to get a piece of paper from Boston to L.A. was by Air Mail—about three days. A few years later, Federal Express and other delivery companies began using sophisticated routing procedures to take paper that distance overnight. Now, I can send a piece of paper across the country in a few seconds with a fax.

Second, while high-technology workers are enhancing communication, they are also broadening it, allowing people to communicate from anywhere to anywhere else. One example of this is the Internet, a complex world-wide network that allows computers to talk to other computers anywhere on the network. This opens enormous possibilities for data sharing and allows people across the globe to communicate with each other via electronic mail (e-mail).

I happen to thrive on my e-mail. I find it on my computer when I go to work in the morning, and I can answer it without having to pick up a pencil or dial a phone. But electronic mail is just one example of the increasing breadth of communications that high-technology workers are giving us. Portable phones, car phones, on-line services like Compuserve and Prodigy, interactive television, electronic bill payment . . . the list could go on and on. The sum of it all is that our opportunities for communication are greater than ever before and will certainly keep increasing faster than we as a society can develop the wisdom to use them.

The dark side of this communications revolution would be obvious if we looked. In the movie *Hook*, Peter Panning is never more than a second away from his business deals because of his cellular phone. It doesn't occur to him that this omnipresence of his business is crowding his family out of his life. Or again, having my home computer on the same network as my computer at work might be a great boon. I might be able to telecommute to work rather than having to drive there. But then will I be able to sort out where my work ends and the rest of my life gets priority?

This ease of communication also has the effect of overloading us with information. Increased access to communication does not necessarily mean increased time to process the information. Nor does it necessarily mean increased care in producing it. For example, the ability to send a fax has not decreased the level of skill necessary to complete a project, the fax has only changed the time required to communicate with others involved in the project.

New communications technologies also create issues of access to information that ought to be private. Fast, easy communication brings with it fast, easy communication of what ought not be made public. Some information about me as a person is sensitive, as is some business information. When computers everywhere are connected, sophisticated crooks can steal information that is not adequately protected.

These are problems that the results of high-technology work in communication bring with them. And yet this is another place where high-technology work is remarkably similar to God's own work. God, it seems, is the great communicator. God wants to communicate with the creation, with people, rather than just sitting alone in divine splendor.

The things we might do to increase communication between people are much in line with God's own work.

And yet for God, communication does not seem to mean flooding the world with data. The apostle Paul says in Ephesians that God hid the plan of redemption until the moment was appropriate to reveal it. This is a sobering realization, for not every piece of information is appropriate for every moment. Some information, it seems, is not ever appropriately communicated. In one of the most bittersweet scenes of the story of Eden, God makes garments to hide the shame of Adam and Eve. I have often thought of that image when I could reveal information about another person that they would rather have left hidden.

This double-edged nature of high-technology work is not limited to communications work. It is everywhere. Although high-technology workers can easily become engrossed in their work for its own sake, it is always worth remembering that it carries costs as well as benefits. As we create novel tools and toys, we create new problems that we will have to find ways of resolving. Knowing this, perhaps we can maintain our sobriety about our inventions and avoid the sin of the nameless engineer who ignored the problems his work created by saying, "I don't drop the bombs, I only build them."

In many important ways, high-technology work is no different from other work. You can be redemptive by redeeming the relationships around you. Unlike farming, which is often a solitary or family task, high-technology work is very team-oriented. These teams can be healthy or not, depending on the quality of the interactions individuals put into them. Good relationships in development teams have to be nurtured. And with all the wild cards that come into them—egos, career plans, customer relations, and the like—a sensitivity to making relationships work is essential to this work.

The relationships between people are a key piece of God's agenda in the workplace. These relationships can be nurtured or nullified by the way we deal with people. So when I go to work, I treat it as the arena in which I will either help or harm the web of relationships. This is a piece of the theology of work that high-technology workers share with everyone else—redemptive working, whether in the cash economy or out of it, whether in high-technology or retailing, means relating redemptively to other people.

Questions for Discussion

1. What do high-technology workers create? Do their products enhance human life or hinder it?

2. Given the complexity of the modern world, what is defense work? Is it problematic for Christians and, if not, why is it such an issue? Would it be any less problematic if it were done in a nonsuperpower country like Switzerland?

3. How does our society learn to deal with the new and innovative? Is it only by trial and error? Or do our mistakes in one area help us to deal with another?

IV.
The Television Journalist:
Telling and Doing the Truth as a Way
of Glorifying God in the Media

Mary Munford

"Jean-Paul Sartre died today. And it doesn't matter." Those words tumbled out of my typewriter one warm spring afternoon in 1980, the day the great French existential philosopher breathed his last. It was a lead that never made air, and was never intended to make air, though it did give my six o'clock producer a chuckle. It served to remind us both not to take ourselves, nor our work, too seriously in the stressful world of television news.

Since that day I have logged more than 24,000 hours in one Los Angeles TV newsroom, going about the serious work of trying to accurately relay the news of the day. And it is serious business. Despite some recent and ominous changes in broadcast news, most TV journalists, like myself, still believe we have a unique calling, a public trust if you will, to provide important and necessary information to the American people. That information helps us all to be better citizens and to lead useful, productive lives.

That conviction has been held by journalists since the very beginnings of what we now call the mass media. A newspaper man who died long before the days of the civil rights movement, the Nixon-Kennedy Debates, or Neil Armstrong's walk on the moon, described it well: Finley Peter Dunne said his job was to "comfort the afflicted and afflict the comfortable."[1] That sounds almost biblical. In fact, it is my personal belief that this journalistic standard is quite in line with Christian faith.

I believe in a God who commands justice and honors truth. Jesus says, "I am the way, the truth and the life."[2] As a follower of Jesus, I believe I am called both to live and to tell the truth, not just in my personal life, but in my professional life as well. I believe this is possible within a career in broadcast journalism, although it is not without its pitfalls.

The Changing Character of Television Broadcasting

An important distinction is necessary: The news organization I work for is not a ministry, not a religious group. Neither is it a nonprofit company nor a humanitarian concern. This seems obvious on the face of it, but still it is tremendously important because, while I share the same goals as the organization I work for, I do not share the same motives.

A television broadcasting concern, whether it is a network or an individual station, is first and foremost a business. Like any other business, it must make a profit if it is to survive. In this sense, ABC, NBC, and CBS are no different than General Motors, McDonald's, or Sears. But there is an added dimension. Broadcasters hold a special position within the business community because they use the public airways to distribute their programs. In a sense, broadcasters are a hybrid—private, for-profit businesses that use the public airways, a limited, natural resource that belongs to the American people. Consequently, broadcasters must be licensed by the Federal Communications Commission. Every few years these licenses come up for renewal, and the owners must prove to the federal regulators that they have been operating in "the public convenience, interest or necessity."[3] To fall short of that standard means to risk the loss of their license.

Because of the licensing requirements and the lucrative nature of entertainment programs, television news historically has held a privileged position within broadcasting. Profits were made primarily through the entertainment side of the business, thus in a sense, subsidizing newsrooms, and to a certain extent, freeing journalists from the forces of the marketplace. Questions of significance, headline value, and the public's need and right to know, were the considerations that determined how and where and to what extent stories were covered. Journalists could afford to be altruistic; they could afford to focus on providing an important public service because the money came from elsewhere in the corporation.

But in the late 1970s, broadcast owners made an important discovery: The public wanted more news, not less. So the owners expanded news programs on the local level to several hours every day, and the money started pouring in. Slowly new questions surfaced: How can we increase the number of our viewers and therefore pump up our profits? And how can we cut the high cost of newsgathering? These newer considerations have not yet replaced the older, traditional questions journalists ask, but a serious competition is now taking place between the two. At an increasing rate, news is beginning to be regarded as a commodity to be sold for profit, rather than as a service to be provided for the public good.

The 1980s brought a major financial setback for broadcasting. The growth of cable and home VCRs siphoned viewers away from the networks. Since 1976, ABC, NBC, and CBS together have lost nearly thirty million viewers, a third of their collective audience. As a result, corporate profits began shrinking in geometric proportions, making it more and more difficult for entertainment programming to subsidize news.[4]

In 1985, the ownership of the three big networks underwent a radical transformation. Capital Cities bought ABC, General Electric swallowed up NBC, and Lawrence Tisch and his Loews corporation began the acquisition of CBS stock that eventually led to controlling interest. Today the three networks are owned by huge conglomerates where broadcasting is only one product among many. This fact alone has changed the corporate culture and the journalistic world for thousands of writers, reporters, producers, and news executives.

As the networks continue to lose ground to cable and home videos, the battle for dwindling audiences rages on. No newsroom and no journalist is immune. The struggle between profit and public interest is here to stay. That is the struggle I have to live with every day.

The Various Shades of Television News

What face does this struggle take? Take a quick look at any local television news broadcast and you'll find stories that range from the trivial to the tremendously important. The Gulf War, presidential politics, the Los Angeles riots, earthquakes, and unemployment. These are important subjects sandwiched in between the latest gossip involving Hollywood stars and British royalty. Not everything that comes across the airwaves is of equal value. The trouble these days, some critics charge, is that the trivial is crowding out the significant. News is becoming less information and more entertainment.

I didn't sign on for this when I first entered the news business in the early seventies. As a child of the sixties, I sat transfixed during those collective moments when television news seemed to bring us all together, whether in the excitement of witnessing a walk on the moon or in the sorrow of watching a caisson carry a fallen president. I watched television news chronicle the Vietnam War, student protests, and the fight for racial equality. And I wanted very much to be a part of that process, in fact to help write current history.

Television news still does this, and often quite well. During times of war, domestic tragedy, and national celebrations we all reach for the dial that will bring us those pictures that often remain seared into our memories. Who can ever forget, for instance, that lone, brave Chinese citizen standing for all the world to see, tiny and solitary, before an entire convoy of Communist tanks near Tianamen Square? More than a thousand newspaper words, that one picture conveyed what it means to struggle to be free.

The power of pictures and the immediacy of the medium often enable television to bring to light important issues that otherwise might go unnoticed. For decades Christian relief organizations and United Nations agencies have been helping the people of Africa with famine relief. But it took a BBC documentary on Ethiopia, which eventually caught the attention of American TV, to turn hunger into an international issue, so compelling that for one Saturday in 1985 the world literally rocked to the sounds of Live Aid, as millions of dollars were raised to help the starving.

Television news is still able to inform and move us in a way that books, newspapers, and magazines, while good in their own way, cannot. I believe that TV news still holds an important place in American society, and I'm glad to be a part of that world.

But there is also a dark side to television. The technology that brings us pictures of inspiration—from the fall of the Berlin Wall to the courage of Magic Johnson publicly facing the specter of HIV—also brings us human depravity at unthinkable levels. More and more local news time is being filled with stories of violence, murder, the bizarre, and all that panders to our voyeuristic tendencies. While some of these stories are important enough to report, when they are played up and promoted to a ridiculous degree, the entire news product is cheapened. But this kind of reporting sells. As a result, ratings go up, broadcasters can then charge advertisers more for airtime, and profits increase. Money is the driving force.

The world of television news is a murky world of conflicting values where profit and the public good are locked in an ongoing struggle. While sometimes the two values coalesce, often they are at odds. Most of the people I work with in the newsroom really do care about providing accurate and useful information to our viewers. Together we struggle to be truthful in what we do, which I believe is honoring to God.

But this is not a simple task. Sometimes we are told to write stories we would rather not do, for example, stories that promote entertainment programs carried by the network. These cross-promotions are self-serving and of very little benefit to the viewer. The 1993 war of the Amy Fishers is a good case in point. All three networks carried so-called "true story" made-for-TV movies of the Long Island, New York scandal in which a young woman goes to prison for shooting the wife of her alleged lover, Joey Buttafuco. All the local news stations then carried "news stories" on their early and late broadcasts, promising their viewers that they would "meet the real people behind the story." The promoted stories carried rehashed information and gratuitous interviews that added nothing new. They were essentially manufactured stories designed to get the viewer to stay with that particular station.

Many journalists have argued against the practice, saying it hurts our credibility and cheapens our professional role as important information providers. But since cross-promotion is a way to increase viewership, and hence profits, all the networks now do it. The practice has become a part of our broadcast life. Fortunately, these types of stories do not make up the majority of news. Not yet.

Since television is a visual medium, it is very much dependent on pictures. A good picture may be worth a thousand words, but in the lingo of television news, a good picture is also worth thousands of dollars. It is a way to get viewers to stay tuned. And this, too, creates a conflict. In 1993 it got NBC into deep trouble with General Motors after the network ran a story showing a GM truck erupting in flames. The network claimed the truck was unsafe, capable of catching fire in the event of an accident; but to illustrate a fiery crash for the camera, rocket lighters were placed under the truck to make certain it would burst into flames. To settle a lawsuit, NBC admitted this piece of staging and issued a long, televised apology. Within that organization, somebody aware of the situation should have sounded the alarm before the story made air. That incident hurt the credibility of all broadcast journalists.

There are, however, many instances the public never hears about when we are able to avoid similar, though maybe not as serious, mistakes. When an editor or writer sees a staging take place, sometimes we can stop it through reasonable debate or, if necessary, heated argument before it ever makes air.

At times I have found myself in that situation. A reporter interviews a crime victim who is afraid for his safety. The reporter promises not to take his picture, but the cameraman surreptitiously takes a picture anyway. Later, the reporter changes his mind and decides to use the picture, by electronically disguising the victim's identity, even though he promised no pictures at all. A videotape editor and I catch the betrayal and convince a producer to drop the picture altogether, thus ensuring the victim's safety and our integrity. We deal with dangerous adversaries to truth on many fronts; one of them is our own desire to get and use the most compelling pictures without regard for the outcome.

The goal of any reputable news organization is to provide reliable information. While the company I work for does this well most of the time, there continues to be an erosion of journalistic values in favor of profit making, a fact that is true for all broadcasting concerns. The company's motive, like every other company, is always profit. As mentioned earlier, often the goal and the motive work well together, but sometimes they are at odds.

The Daily Goals of a News Producer

As a journalist my goal is the same as that of my company's: To participate faithfully in the information process. But as a Christian, my motive goes far beyond that of simply collecting a paycheck. There are wider issues at stake.

Scripture teaches us that we are not our own, that we were bought with a price, therefore work cannot be just a solitary, individual endeavor to make money. God has a claim on all of my life, including the one-third I spend in the workplace. As Christians there is a collective quality to our lives that embraces even the work that we do. Certainly, I work to support myself, but as a Christian I am also called to glorify God with my life, including the hours between nine and five.

Johann Sebastian Bach, upon completion of a work of music, would often initialize each new manuscript "sdg," the Latin shorthand for *Soli Deo Gloria*, for the glory of God. Nearly 300 years later, his efforts still provide an example for us all. Bach produced his work to make a living, but he did it ultimately for God, including the music that was not directly ecclesiastical. This, I believe, is a pattern for all Christians.

Now I don't write sermons. In fact, the vast majority of my writing could not even be classified as inspirational, although I hope that the words I write would inspire people to listen carefully to the information being given. My topics include the consumer price index, the latest labor figures, as well as the standard news stories of violence and pain—from traffic accidents and fires to yet another gang-related shooting some-where in the social amalgam known as Los Angeles.

So how can this be to the glory of God?

First, we live in a culture that depends on information. Each morn-ing, for instance, people want and need to know what the weather is going to be like, and in Southern California the place where I work, they need to know about traffic congestion and major accidents so they can take alternate routes to work. It is a big city fact of life. Television news also provides important consumer information in the areas of health, medicine, and economics. In the realm of politics, it is a working journa-listic article of faith that an informed electorate is an absolute essential for the well functioning of any democracy.

By writing these types of stories, my work is similar to that of any farmer, truck driver, seamstress, or shoemaker who provides necessary goods and services. This is valuable work in and of itself because it helps to sustain other peoples' lives. And it corresponds with God's own providential care for and service to the creation in all kinds of active, everyday ways. To do this well, accurately, and with integrity, is one way to glorify God on the job.

Second, this activity benefits me as well. As a journalist I use my gifts to enrich others, to help improve their lives by empowering them with information, which in turn ties me into the community of others. It keeps me from being self-focused because I do not speak into a dark-ened, silent sky. My words have meaning because they can be a vehicle to benefit others, even when those words do not deal directly with spiritual reality.

This corresponds well with God's own communal character and activities. Doing work that places me within the larger society of God's creation is another way to glorify the God whose kingdom will one day be established on earth.

Third, in addition to "speaking the truth" by providing useful information, journalists also have the opportunity to "reveal the truth." It is their responsibility to uncover information about corruption, mismanagement, and injustice. Muckraking holds a long and honorable tradition within journalism, from the early days of newspapers to *60 Minutes*. In fact, the term *muckraking* has a distinctively Christian history, now lost to most journalists. The term entered the American vernacular in a 1906 speech by President Theodore Roosevelt when he referred to the man with a muck rake in John Bunyon's *Pilgrim's Progress.*[5]

Over and over again the Bible reveals a God who calls us both to do and to love justice. To reveal injustice, then, is yet another way of remaining faithful and bringing glory to God.

Fourth, the work of a journalist is creative. I deal with facts that need to be communicated, but there is more than one way to tell a story accurately. In television, we work not only with words, but also with pictures and sound. While I believe I am called to tell the truth, I have to get at this truth by choosing selectively; I have to decide what goes on the air and what doesn't. My raw material often consists of several pages of facts and several minutes worth of video, all of which may have to be distilled into a thirty-second news story.

This kind of work constitutes part of the creative process. And since the God we worship is the Creator, who has given us all the ability to create, this too is part of doing God's work and glorifies our Creator.

Finally, my work is contemplative. The information that I gather and must then turn around into a news story, is information that comes to me from the outside world. But the process of turning that information around, the creative process of making sense out of it all, is an internal process that engages not only my mind but my heart. There is a moment right as I sit down at my computer, before any words spill forth, where I face a severe emptiness. What am I going to say? How am I going to say it? Will it be any good? That moment may last only a second or two, but it is a moment tinged with fear as well as excitement because I never know exactly what is going to come out.

When the words do flow, I experience pleasure, a little rush, perhaps even a tinge of joy. This discipline of contemplation, and the experience of joy that comes from entering into it, reminds me that I am ultimately dependent on God.

Conclusion

I am not proud of everything that goes out on our airwaves. Much of it disturbs and distresses me. But for now, I am convinced that it is better for me to stay within the system, flawed though it is, attempting to be faithful in the things I can do, staying alert to new possibilities for change, and yet recognizing that some things are quite beyond my control.

When I am present in that situation, attempting to both tell and expose the truth; when I show up every day, briefcase in hand, hopeful for the opportunity to use my creative skills to benefit others; and when I experience the deep pleasure that comes from using the gifts God has given me, then I know that what I do in the workplace is indeed an act of faith, and as such, brings glory to God.

There is a wider meaning to this work that I do because I serve a greater audience who has blessed me with a serious, though joyful, responsibility.

Jean Paul Sartre died, and it does, indeed, matter. It matters every day.

Notes

1. F. P. Dunne, *Mr. Dooley At His Best* (New York: Charles Scribner & Sons, 1938), 228.

2. John 14:6.

3. Sydney W. Head, *Broadcasting in America* (Boston: Houghton Mifflin, 1976), 323.

4. K. Auletta, *Three Blind Mice: How the Networks Lost Their Way* (New York: Random House, 1991) 7.

5. 1 Cor. 6:20.

6. Edwin Emery, *The Press and America* (Englewood Cliffs: Prentice-Hall, 1972), 384.

Questions for Discussion

1. How does the practice of "truth-telling" affect your own occupation? Are there ways in which your workplace engages in misinformation, deception, even lies?

2. When is it appropriate to make compromises in this area? When is it important to stand up for the truth?

3. Are there opportunities within your own occupation to help improve other people's lives, work for justice, nurture your own creativity, and attempt to live a contemplative life?

4. As a consumer, are you frustrated with television news and entertainment programming? Are you willing to work for change in this area?
   If so, since under FCC regulations all correspondence to broadcasters must be read and kept in a special file, write a letter and express your views.

   — Address it to either the station's News or Program Director.

   — List the program, date, time, and channel. Then briefly, but specifically, state your concern.

   — Limit your letter to one page. Be polite and avoid inflammatory language. Let them know you are a reasonable person with reasonable concerns.

   If you want to go a step further:

   — Note the program's advertisers and locate their corporate offices.

   — Send a copy of your letter to the advertisers, making sure to list their names in a c.c. note on the bottom of your original letter to the broadcaster. This will get everyone's attention!

V.
The Builder-Developer as a Steward of God's Resources: Bringing God's Kingdom to the Marketplace and Inner City

Perry Bigelow

There are two ways to connect faith and work. One can integrate faith into work, in which case faith is secondary to work, or one can integrate work into faith, in which case faith is primary. I have tried both ways. For me integrating faith into work resulted in compartmentalization; integrating work into faith is holistic. All work done in Jesus' name and done for Jesus (Col. 3:23-24) is part of the good work that God has created me to do—whether it is work in the marketplace, in the community, at home, or at church.

The Incarnation: The Central Mystery

I shall never understand fully the mystery of the incarnation. First, God's Son was incarnated in a human body 2,000 years ago (Jn. 1:1-5, 10-14). Second, He is incarnated in me (Rom. 8:9-11; Eph. 1:1-14). Third, in a way that only God understands, He is incarnated and present in the poor and needy person. When I reach out and provide shelter to the stranger, a drink to the thirsty, or something to eat for the hungry, I am providing that to Jesus (Mt. 25:31-46). This puts an incredibly awesome significance on reaching out to those in need. In some mystical way I am also the incarnation of Jesus to the poor; He serves the poor through me. And he who is poor at any given time is the incarnation of Jesus to me.[1] As a result, in each encounter with any person, I have the opportunity simultaneously to be Jesus the rich person, as a giver of God's grace, and Jesus the poor person, as a receiver of God's grace. Lately, I also have come to realize that I am often the poor person, therefore, if I want to receive the full blessing of Jesus' incarnation for myself, I must be humble and vulnerable enough to allow other people to be Jesus to me.

God's Image: The Dignity of Making Decisions

Jesus fully respected the image of God that each person carries; from His encounters with people it is evident that an essential element of that image is the freedom and ability to make responsible choices. Therefore, in all my interpersonal relationships, I must not participate as a person of power but as a person who offers to another God's gift of decision-making ability. In our company we have a concept of leading people and managing assets. It is almost impossible to manage people without falling into the trap of treating them like an "it" instead of a "thou."

Jesus never exerted His supernatural power over people against their will or against what they perceived to be their own self-interest. Primary examples are Zaccheus (Lk. 19:1-9) and the Rich Young Ruler (Lk. 18:18-25). Both were wealthy but one accepted His call, the other rejected it. I must allow people the same dignity of decision. Since I am not naturally people-oriented, it has become a difficult, but wonderfully exciting life-long journey to learn to try to provide everyone I encounter with that God-given privilege. I am not even close to doing this consistently.

Inverted Megacultures:
The Kingdoms of God and This World

As followers of Jesus, we are participants and citizens of two opposite megacultures. The kingdom of God is where God reigns; the kingdom of this world is all that has not submitted itself to God's rule. Because evidence of our vertical relationship with God is not yet visible, His kingdom is seen only in our horizontal relationships. The earthly kingdom has its own economic, social, and political systems that are almost always totally upside down to the relational systems of God's kingdom and culture. At this point I have a great deal of difficulty as a Christian business owner. For example, laws are written so that everyone is treated the same, but God loves diversity and makes each person unique. It is often difficult to respond to each person's uniqueness in a legally-bound business environment. Also, whereas the state says that Christians own their own businesses, Christians view themselves as merely trustees or stewards of God's kingdom assets.

Biblical Perspectives on Work

In the Roman social and economic system, slavery was the primary employer-employee relationship. Stewards or managers were often highly educated, well-trained slaves who were completely entrusted with their owner's property. There is a close correlation between the way these people handled their master's wealth in Jesus' parables and the way a business owner should handle the assets of the company, as well as between the way masters and slaves related to one another and the way employers and employees should operate today.[2]

We are God's workmanship created in Christ Jesus to do good works which God prepared that we might walk in them (Eph. 2:10). This is an extremely important truth because it defines what I am to do as a result of the gracious gift of salvation that I have received from God (Eph. 2:8-9). In Greek, "workmanship" has the connotation of a complete piece of woven fabric or a work of art. I am God's good, complete, divine work of art. Due to God's ability to see the end at the beginning, I am already viewed as the perfect likeness of Jesus (Rom. 8:28-29). The good works that occupy me form the substance of my "doing" and "working" day in and day out.

Just what are these?[3] They include all kinds of work—physical, social, and ethical. They involve general behavior (Tit. 2:7), providing for daily necessities (Tit. 3:14), and sharing of wealth (1 Tim. 6:17-19)[4] So good works are the totality of what God has prepared for me to do. They include my professional calling as an entrepreneur and home-builder; my treatment of employees, customers, and suppliers; my reaching out and touching the poor; and activities that result from my being part of Jesus' body, the church. There is no compartmentalization between secular work in the marketplace and Christian serving. All of a Christian's life and work is ministry; all is to be done in the name of Jesus, as to Jesus, and for the glory of Jesus.

My Personal Journey

God's Invasion of My Life

I have not always had this understanding of work. For many years I had a very compartmentalized idea of faith and a highly secularized view of work. On the one hand, people needed to be saved, and I had a responsibility to witness to them. On the other hand, people were factors in capital investment and potential productivity, and I had to manage them to maximize my economic return. I became a master manipulator. I started the business to make money, not to build the capital base of God's kingdom. I even had the audacity to invite God to be my partner—who would get a fair share for blessing me. I spent a lot of my spare time ensuring that I had a secure future by acquiring and growing my real estate investments, placing my confidence in these, rather than God. At the same time I taught Sunday School, was the church trustee board chairman, and directed the construction of some of our church buildings. There was little connection between my Sunday faith and my Monday work.

What changed? Four things happened. First, God graciously used a severe depression in the housing industry to show me that there is no lasting or real security to be found in owning a business or owning investments. As a result I developed a strong desire to know God better, to trust God more, and to feel loved by God. Second, just as this desire was intensifying, in Sunday School we studied Richard Foster's book *Celebration of Discipline*. For the first time in my life I began to practice seriously the spiritual disciplines of Bible study, meditation, and prayer —typically one half hour to one hour in the morning, and fifteen to thirty minutes in the evening.[5] Third, I read James Sheldon's book *In His Steps*, a story about a spiritually shallow pastor and his congregation and how their lives were revolutionized in one year by asking one simple question before anything they did: "What would Jesus do?" Fourth, I read Charles Colson's autobiographies, *Born Again* and *Life Sentence*, and was shamed by the realization that he was much closer to God after being a Christian for only a few years than I was after thirty years.

As a result of this confluence of events and intensive study of the Bible, I realized that it was spiritually dangerous to be economically rich.[6] I also realized that I had to make a choice between God and money

(Mt. 6:24). I became so horrified of the spiritual risk of being wealthy that I told God that if it was just the same with Him, I'd like never to be rich—the risk was just too great. Before, I feared God and loved money: having decided to really love God I developed a healthy fear of money. I sold all my investments; I have nothing left except my house—no stocks, mutual funds, or other retirement-type accounts.

I also came to realize that Jesus deeply loved and showed proactive concern for the poor, so much so that in His only story about who is allowed to enter the kingdom, it is only those who have directly and personally fed, clothed, and entertained the poor who will be welcomed (Mt. 25:31-46). This was truly shocking because I didn't know any poor in my cloistered, affluent suburban lifestyle. I began looking for ways to touch Jesus by touching the poor. I began to understand how much God hates oppression and loves justice.[7] Finally I concluded that I was a *de facto* oppressor. I was not proactively *for* justice like God was; I was doing nothing to provide just opportunity for victims of structural oppression.

I toyed with the idea of closing the homebuilding business so that I could become heavily involved with the poor; ultimately I decided to grow the homebuilding company as a means of support. I gathered around me highly competent leaders who could manage the business on a day-to-day basis. This has provided me with the financial support and the personal time necessary to become involved in a wide range of activities that come alongside people in the city, with those who want to help themselves.

My Basic Criterion—
How Would Jesus Think and What Would Jesus Do?

I continuously ask the question: What kind of a homebuilding company would Jesus establish and own?

I believe Jesus would build homes that satisfy a family's needs, not its luxuries. The homes would be of durable quality; they would have natural beauty, not status beauty; they would be resource-efficient to build and maintain; they would be designed to enhance family life; and they would provide the opportunity to develop interdependent, neighborly relationships.

I believe Jesus would appeal to good, human qualities in His marketing; He would not appeal to greed, covetousness, status, pride, etc. He would honestly state the advantages of His homes. By the way, our commitment to be honest in advertising has consistently driven us to build better homes than our competition—nobody wants to advertise that his home is average.

I believe Jesus, as the owner of the business, would pray the only prayer about wealth in the Bible: "Give me neither poverty nor riches, but give me only my daily bread. Otherwise I may have too much and disown you and say, 'Who is the Lord?'" (Pr. 30:8-9). A shortened version of this prayer is included in the prayer Jesus taught His disciples: "Give us today our daily bread" (Mt. 6:11).

He would certainly follow His own advice about not storing up treasure for ourselves on earth but in heaven (Mt. 6:19-20), not worrying about food or clothing for tomorrow (Mt. 6:25-34), and not building bigger barns in which to hoard His Father's resources (Lk. 12:16-21).

I believe Jesus would capitalize His business responsibly so that His employees could have steady employment. Following God's concern for more equal distribution of resources (2 Cor. 8:13-14), the balance of His profits would be invested in helping the poor and spreading the Gospel (1 Tim. 6:17-19). He probably would not hoard, save, or invest profits outside the capital needs of the business (Lk. 12:16-21). He would practice justice and equality in paying wages and sharing profit with employees (Col. 4:1).

I am an entrepreneur, and I am a homebuilder. I own and lead a suburban homebuilding company, and I am an entrepreneur in inner city activities involving housing as well as economic and human development activities in the inner city. By nature, I am an entrepreneur, as was my father. I love to start things; I love to innovate. I am good at analyzing risk and future potential; I can handle the stress of risk-taking.

I am not, by nature, a good manager or organizer, so we have highly skilled leaders in each functional business area (marketing, design, construction, finance, purchasing) who are responsible for the day-to-day activities of the company. We meet weekly and make planning, personnel, policy, and procedural decisions by consensus. There is a high degree of camaraderie and mutual respect and, except for issues involving Christian ethics, I submit myself to the consensual process as do all the others. This consensual approach to leadership is partly a result of my understanding of my responsibility to be just and to foster equality. Even though some of the leaders are not believers, this group has been able to provide mutual accountability. This consensual approach provides what Max DePree calls the "space . . . to exercise our gifts and diversity."[8]

The biblical model for co-participation and fellowship is the body (Rom. 12:3-8; 1 Cor. 12:4-29). So long as people are committed to a common goal, the body is a better metaphor for business organization than the typical hierarchical organization chart. There is still hierarchy but interdependence, collaboration, and consensus are emphasized. This body metaphor and consensual interdependence pervades the relationships within each operating area and across all areas of the company. There are no private kingdoms in our company; no one builds moats or gates, and no one is a gatekeeper. Each person's work is integrated and interrelated with the work of others, and there is a high level of respect for each person's contribution.

A person's dignity and self-esteem will not be enhanced by their work unless they can see how their work either directly or indirectly results in the production and distribution of a quality product or service. Therefore there must be a highly visible trail between an employee's work, the home we build, and the purchaser of that home. This trail is made visible through the human interrelationships involved in each person's contribution. Our broad-based mutual accountability and interrelatedness results in a culture that develops strong, independent people with a high level of mutual self-respect. It is a satisfying culture within which to work. One of our leaders often says he has the best of all worlds: he loves to come to work in the morning, and he loves to go home at night. It is not unusual to have a first-time visitor to our office say something like "It's so peaceful here; everyone is so content."

We feel that we have a responsibility to provide steady employment. This is very difficult to do since the homebuilding industry is extremely cyclical. It is not unusual for housing starts in a given market to drop by sixty to eighty percent in a short time. We have a threefold strategy to stabilize employment. First, we invest heavily in information systems that result in very high individual productivity. Second, in good times we do not expand as rapidly as we could. Third, we have no goal to be big for the sake of being big. We aim for careful, sustainable growth. This combination allowed us to go through the last Chicago housing cycle without laying off anyone, while many homebuilders were reducing their staffs by fifty to seventy percent.

Because we recognize that a person who joins our firm must operate within the business culture we have created, we take the employment interviewing process very seriously. We want to make sure that new employees will fit well with our group and have full knowledge of our approach to business, so that they can make good decisions as to whether they will enjoy working with us. This interview process involves several meetings and usually stretches over several weeks. By the time they are hired, new employees feel like they are known, that they are respected for their skills, that both strengths and weaknesses have been acknowledged, and that they will be treated with dignity and respect. All full-time employees go through the same interview process, whether they will be a vice president or a receptionist.

Our people are so important to us that no personnel decision is made until there is full consensus by the leadership group. Every employee is told that the owner of the company operates the company on basic biblical principles, which means that the truth will always be spoken in love (Eph. 4:15) and that we shall never knowingly lie to each other, a home purchaser, a supplier or subcontractor, or government official. We place a high premium on personal integrity, and we want potential employees to know that they will not enjoy working with us if they do not have what Covey calls the character ethic of integrity and principle-centered leadership.[9] One of the results of this fastidious honesty is that over time people outside our company have come to trust our employees implicitly.

We use biblical principles of body interdependence and *koinonia* (fellowship and co-participation) in the design of our communities. In his book *Habits of the Heart,* Robert Bellah has observed that there must be a careful balance between individualism and interdependence to maintain democratic, neighborly-oriented lifestyles.[10] Suburban communities have lost that balance; they have become extremely individualistic. The way builders relate homes to the street and each other today almost precludes the development of natural neighborliness between families. Our communities restore a balance between privacy and neighborliness, and they result in natural opportunities to interact in a neighborly way.

We have received a national reputation for building innovative, highly energy-efficient homes with a guarantee that the heating bills will not exceed $200 per year in Chicago. Our innovation in energy efficiency is a direct result of our great respect for God's creation and a belief that we should preserve as much of it as we can for our children's children. We strive to preserve the natural beauty of land as we plan and develop it. I do not see how a believer can be anything other than an environmentalist; it is only responsible stewardship to cherish and respect what God graciously has given us.

In the Inner City

I enjoy my work in the inner city as much as my work in the suburbs. You could say that we make money in the suburbs and spend it in the inner city. I became deeply involved in working with economically poor people in the inner city by asking these questions: What would Jesus do? Where would Jesus invest or spend His Father's resources? How would Jesus practice equality? Where would Jesus live?

I now live in an African-American community in Chicago's inner city, and the church I now call home is predominately African-American. Originally I became involved because Jesus called me, not because "I" wanted to. In hindsight, as a result of the joy of the work I do and the joy of where I live and worship, I'd do it now for the joy because of the rich relationships I have. I am loved, nurtured, and cared about there. I am not saying that all believers should live among the economically poor, however, it does seem odd that the vast preponderance of those who have an economic choice and who have Jesus in their hearts ask only the question: "Where amongst the rich should I live?" instead of "Where amongst *all* of God's people does He want me to live?"

There is not enough space here to develop fully the biblical presuppositions surrounding my work and life in the inner city, however, I shall explain briefly the principles and the work I do.

The biblical presuppositions are as follows:

Jubilee. God instituted an economic system in Israel that was designed to provide an even distribution of the economic resources necessary to live a Godly life. Although Jubilee rewarded industriousness and penalized sluggardness, there was no way individuals could become excessively and extravagantly wealthy. Part of the plan was a redistribution system preventing any family from becoming permanently impoverished due to economic adversity or individual laziness (Dt. 15; Lev. 25:8-43). Jesus extended this principle further, involving a degree of giving and sharing that can only be fully actualized in kingdom relationships.

Equality. Paul encouraged the churches to practice economic equality (2 Cor. 8:1-9:15). Those who have God's resources are to share so thoroughly and deeply that they run the risk of becoming impoverished themselves (2 Cor. 8:14) as Jesus did (2 Cor. 8:9).

Calling. God has provided a "good work" for every believer to do (Eph. 2:10). Unfortunately many people have been deprived of the capital, training, and personal resources necessary to accomplish that good work. Those of us who are stewards of God's resources must make sure that they are fully shared and that all believers have the opportunity and resources to do the good work God has called them to do.

Gleaning. The principle of gleaning involves providing others with the opportunity to help themselves. In Israel, able-bodied people were to be given the opportunity to provide for themselves from what others produced. The story of Ruth and Boaz is the perfect example of this principle at work.

Justice. God loves justice and hates oppression (Is. 58; Am. 5; Jas. 5:1-6).

I used to see myself as a self-made individualist, having come from an economically poor background. I forgot about a loving father who, by his example, instilled in me a positive attitude of hope; a mother who deeply loved God; an older sister who deeply loved me; a brother who counseled me; innumerable friends who stood by me; people who mentored me; and a country of opportunity, a superb educational system, etc. I selected almost none of these; they are all gifts of God through others' investments in me. Except for these opportunities (over which I had no control) I'd be among the poorest of the poor, both spiritually and physically.

God says: Invest in the poor as I have invested in you. I am God's steward of those investments—of those good works. When I see everything I am and have as God's gift and stewardship, and when I hear God shout jubilee, grace, equality, sharing, and justice, I cannot claim any of that wealth for my own; the entrepreneurial and building skills, the networking and financial resources, are all God's to be shared fully with others. It is helping others help themselves so they can help others—like others helped me so I could help others.

I am participating in the cycle of reinvestment and helping to stop the cycle of disinvestment in the inner city. I use investment and reinvestment in the broadest sense to include spiritual, economic, social, institutional, moral, as well as personal time, mentoring, youth development, business and professional networks, technical skills, and any other kind of investment you can imagine. We have the ability and the perseverance to be "seed hope" and "seed capital" to see an opportunity through to completion.

Everything we are involved in in the inner city is a joint venture or partnership with either a church or a church-related community development group. We do nothing by ourselves. We help low income working people build their own high quality, energy efficient homes. We provide organizational expertise, seed capital, hope, technical design, construction management, land development, risk taking and entrepreneurial skills, purchasing networks, and financial resources, but the people are building the homes themselves. We coordinate the efforts of people from all walks of life: accountants, carpenters, lawyers, electricians, business owners, plumbers, and truck drivers. Our objective is to make kingdom resources available to kingdom people.

I make all of the resources of the suburban homebuilding company available to the work in the inner city, except for the employees themselves. Inner city work is not, and cannot be, a condition of employment for the employees, many of whom are not believers. However, all of the business networks, technical skills and knowledge, and financial resources, are fully available to be shared.

Conclusion

I walk down life's path continually asking the questions: How would Jesus think? What would Jesus do? I know that I am the workmanship of God and that He has provided a whole range of good work for me to do. All of the good work I do is blessed and is a blessing to me and to others, whether it is designing and building homes and neighborhoods in the suburbs or recapitalizing and rebuilding the inner city, whether it is respecting the image of God and the incarnation of Jesus in an employee, customer, or friend or mentoring and modeling Jesus' incarnation in decaying urban centers. It is the highest joy and honor to give back to Jesus as much as I can of what He has given to me.

Can you feel their pain, has it touched your life?
Can you taste the salt in the tears they cry?
Will you love them more than the hate that's been?
Will you love them back to life again?[11]

Notes

All Bible references are from the New International Version or my own paraphrases.

1. This aspect of Christian faith is best lived, practiced, and written by Tony Campolo in *A Reasonable Faith: Responding to Secularism* (Waco: Word, 1983), 172-178.

2. Paul uses the same word (*kyrios*) for earthly master or lord and for Jesus, our heavenly Master and Lord.

3. They are described in 2 Cor. 9:8; Col. 1:10; 2 Th. 2:17; Phil. 1:6; I Tim. 2:10, 5:10, 5:25, 6:18; 2 Tim. 2:21, 3:17; Tit. 1:16, 2:7 and 14, 3:1,8,14; Heb. 10:24; I Pet. 2:12.

4. See further I Tim. 6:5b-8 and then 1 Tim. 6:9-10.

5. My simple method of daily Bible study involves writing down the answers to three questions: 1) *What does it say?* This is a paraphrase of the verse(s) that takes into consideration the meaning of the surrounding verses. 2) *What does it mean?* I jot down what the key words mean, what the key thoughts are, and anything else that I learn about the passage. 3) *What does it mean to me?* I write down how the passage affects me and what I need to do about it. This is often in the form of prayers of thanksgiving, of praise, and requests for God's help in changing my attitudes and actions.

6. Jas. 2:5-7, 5:1-6; I Tim. 6:9-10; Mt. 19:16-26. James' diatribes against the wealthy and Jesus' warning to the rich made me realize that I was playing with a dangerous explosive that could destroy me. I had read these verses many times and intellectually had rationalized away their truth. How easy it was to see the truth when I really wanted to listen to God.

7. Am. 2:6-7, 4:1-6, 5:7, 10-24, 6:3-8, 8:4-12; Is. 1:15-17, 5:8-9, 58:1-14

8. Max DePree, *Leadership is an Art* (New York: Doubleday, 1989), 7, 14. This is an excellent book.

9. Stephen R. Covey, *Principle-Centered Leadership* (New York: Simon andSchuster, 1992). Stephen Covey has written this and another excellent book on leadership: *7 Habits of Highly Effective People* (New York: Simon and Schuster, 1989).

10. Robert Bellah, *Habits of the Heart: Individualism and Commitment in American Life* (New York: Harper & Row, 1985), chapter 3.

11. *Do You Feel Their Pain?* Words by Steve Camp, Phill McHugh, Rob Frazier, and Kim Maxfield-Camp; music by Steve Camp.

Questions for Discussion

1. How could applying the principle of offering others "God's gift of making decisions" change one's approach to their work?

2. In what ways has the desire to accumulate wealth influenced your spiritual choices? If you were to change your attitudes about wealth, how would that affect your role in the workplace? (See Jas. 2:5-7; 5:1-6; 1 Tim.6:9-10; Mt. 6:24; 19:16-26.)

3. How would your work be changed if you asked yourself: "What would Jesus think and what would Jesus do?" before making your decisions?

4. How could you apply the biblical principles of jubilee, equality, calling, gleaning, and justice to your present work?

VI.
A Business Owner's Mission: Working as a Christian in a Car Sales Firm

Don Flow

What follows is an outgrowth of my own personal quest, a quest for which I have great passion: To bring integration to my faith and work, or more accurately, to have my faith transform my work. I have attempted to develop a biblical theology that creates the foundation for understanding my life in the marketplace and a coherent world view that can be articulated in a workplace setting. From this framework I have derived relevant managerial and organizational principles for my automobile dealerships.

The Threefold Call of Christ

The biblical concept of vocation provides the foundation for understanding how our life in God is to unfold. The call of Christ is the most profound event in human experience—it is regenerating, redefining, and refocusing. The call of Jesus Christ is a threefold one, one call with three dimensions. The first dimension of the call of Christ is to *salvation*. When Jesus calls us to Himself, we are forgiven and saved from the consequences of our sins. This call is the most personal experience that anyone will know. The second dimension of the call of Christ is *sanctification* to personal holiness. We are called to put on a new self, to be transformed. His call redefines the values in our life. The third dimension of the call is to *service*, an other-centered life. This refocuses our energy and resources from our self to others as we respond to the life-altering question: "How does our life bear witness to Jesus Christ who came to serve?" As Lee Hardy says, the call of Christ is "not to leave the world behind to live the life of faith, but to live the life of faith in the midst of the world."

In every sphere of life, we must work out that call. And that three-fold call must be held together as a unity. When the call is fractured, with one dimension being the single focus, we will live a truncated, frag-mented life. When reduced to salvation only, the call easily becomes believism or cheap grace. The profoundly personal call becomes more like the rush of adrenaline—a powerful short-term burst of energy that doesn't last. It does not transform our lives, it rarely has an impact on our relationships, and its imprint on our character is generally quite temporary.

When the call by Christ is reduced to sanctification, the call is diminished to moralism. Our relationship with the living God is lost and we hold onto the form of faith by adhering to a moral code. Because this moral code is not an outgrowth of the grace of God, behavior becomes self-righteous.

When reduced to service, the call by Christ easily becomes activism. When this happens our lives are no longer energized by the inner renewal of the Holy Spirit. Rather, we become driven by the need to do some-thing significant. In doing so, we lose our witness for Christ.

Our call does not come in a vacuum and it does not call us into a vacuum. Our call comes in a specific personal place and it puts us or leaves us in a specific personal place. The call of Christ comes to each of us in a particular culture with a defined sphere of relationships and with certain preferences and desires.

When Christ calls us, we are restored and renewed to what we were *meant* to be. We are more than just an improved edition of who we *used* to be. Like Saul of Tarsus, Jesus gives us a new name, one that gives ultimate purpose and meaning to our existence. Jesus Christ opens to us the path to the fulfillment of our reason for existence: communion with God, community with one another, and co-creation with God in the world (2 Cor. 5:17-20).

When we respond to the call of Christ, we begin a new journey in which we are not divested of our self. Instead, we begin the process of bringing to completion what we were created to be. As we are faithful to that calling, we find ourselves being transformed in a way that might well be a source of astonishment not only to others, but also to ourselves. This is a recognition that the God of the universe is able to do immeasurably more than we ask or imagine our lives. To paraphrase Karl Barth: We will never know in advance where the call of Christ will lead us in our journey.

A word of caution: The call that comes to us in a specific place is not to be confused with the place itself. We can be led by the Holy Spirit to a specific place to live out our vocation. But our vocation remains the same in every sphere of life—total faithfulness to Jesus Christ. Our job is not our vocation. To say that God's calling is the same as our employment would reduce the call to the impulse to work. How we live faithfully for Christ in that specific employment is our vocation, transcending our work.

The outworking of this faithfulness cannot be reduced to a formula. Our response to the call is shaped by the interaction of the opportunities for service in a particular place, our unique personal gifts and temperament, and the movement of the Holy Spirit in a particular moment. Being called to Christ and by Christ means that in every context of life we must seek to work out our salvation, sanctification, and service. Having been called from death to life, we are called to be without blemish, and to live a life of spiritual service to the world under the guidance of the Holy Spirit.

As we seek to live faithfully for Christ, ordinary time can give way to redemptive time in every sphere of life. It is at this moment that all of us have the potential to exercise a priestly ministry: touching people for God and touching God on behalf of people. It is in this place where faith, hope, and love move from doctrine to life. The spiritual sacrifice of service to others, offered through a life congruent with the Beatitudes and empowered by the Holy Spirit, provides the avenue for work to be transformed into something sacred. Our temporal efforts in this world are infused with eternal significance as we seek to exercise our gifts and talents for our neighbor's sake and the kingdom of God.

Governing Commitments

Bringing definition to our call or making it real for a specific place in life means responding to three profound questions. Why? What? How? The response to these three questions represent what I call the governing commitments in our life. The answer to why is the purpose or reason for

our existence. The answer to the question of what is vision—the picture
of the future we seek to create. While purpose and mission represent a
direction, vision leads to a specific destination. Purpose is at the foundation of our being. Vision wells up from within us and finds expression in
the specifics of life. Purpose is abstract, vision is concrete. A vision
with no underlying sense of purpose cannot be sustained because it fails
to address fundamental reasons for existence. Our core values define
how we will act and live as we pursue our vision.

These governing commitments also are applicable to organizations.
I have implemented the governing commitments in my dealerships and
have found that the explicit recognition and integration of purpose,
vision, and core values must take place for an organization to flourish.

Focusing on the governing commitments of organizational life
forces us together to answer "What do we believe?" The energy that
comes when an organization commits to a purpose, vision, and core
values derives from the power of these governing commitments to fulfill
intrinsic desires for meaning that transcend specific economic goals.
These desires have the power to call forth a level of commitment and
dedication that creates a common identity among diverse people.

I have used the concept of governing commitments to make explicit
my calling from Jesus Christ, to live faithfully for Him in every sphere of
life. Each sphere of life must be addressed with its own set of governing
commitments if we are to live purposefully for Jesus Christ. Because
purpose focuses on our very reason for existence, my purpose is the same
for every sphere of life. The way that purpose finds expression changes
with the vision and core values that apply in each sphere. My vision
brings definition to my call in a particular place and my core values are
the point of tangible integration.

My personal workplace vision statement, what I want to be, is not a
final statement. My identity before God is not static and the circumstances in which He has placed me are always evolving.

> To articulate and embody a vision of our organization as a commu-
> nity of uniquely gifted people whose life together is characterized by
> grace and truth and whose reason for existence is to serve others.

In this statement are three core values that I believe bear witness to
Jesus Christ. This is the point of integration for me in my work life. It is

how my calling from Christ takes on real meaning. These three values are: extraordinary service to others, the development of people, and community building.

Extraordinary Service to Others

Extraordinary service to others is consonant with the words of Jesus: "Whoever wants to become great among you must be your servant, just as the Son of Man did not come to be served, but to serve" (Mt. 20:26-28). If the primary character attribute of Jesus was that of service, then this characteristic should dominate my behavior as well. As the president of the company, it is my goal that this be the defining attribute of the entire organization. Our goal of service to others is the very foundation of our purpose for existence. Consequently, this focus is captured in our company's mission statement: "To deliver an extraordinary level of service at every point of contact with the customer in a personal and professional manner."

We debated and agonized over every word in this statement. One of the benefits of being the owner of a company is that there is great opportunity for congruence between personal governing commitments and corporate governing commitments. Nonetheless, ownership of the capital does not imply ownership of the mission. For a corporate mission to be a living reality, it must be fully integrated into the organizational culture.

The mission statement creates the foundation for developing the shared vision of our company. To make this vision a reality, there must be a common language that conveys the emotive dimension of the vision. Development of that common language is my responsibility.

To accomplish this, I meet with employees daily, one-on-one and in groups. I ask them how I can help them fulfill our vision. Our common language includes words and phrases such as: exceeding customer's expectations, going the extra mile, giving of ourselves, being there for our customers, building trust, developing relationships, serving when it is not convenient, and creating customer enthusiasm.

In addition, we define our success in how we have served our customers. We survey customers after they have purchased vehicles or received service. Roughly one-third of our employees' compensation depends on customers' perceptions of service.

We think that declaring our intentions to the customer is important because that holds us accountable to the vision. Once we have declared our standards, they provide the norm for defining our progress towards the vision.

One of the ways we declare standards to ourselves and to our customers is to post our commitments throughout the dealerships. We review with every customer our promise to them. For instance, in our service departments, we have a commitment board that is prominently positioned for every customer to read. It states:

Our Commitment to You!

1. To properly diagnose and repair your vehicle on the first visit to the dealership. If we fail to do so, we will provide you with substitute transportation. We will return your vehicle to you totally cleaned and vacuumed.

2. To provide you with an estimate before we begin the repairs on your car. If we fail to do so, we will repair your car at no charge.

3. To repair your vehicle for the price promised. If we exceed the amount you authorize, we will pay for it. No questions asked.

4. To complete your repairs when we promise. If we fail to do so, we will provide you with transportation while we finish the repairs.

These are just a few of the examples of our efforts to strive to make our vision a reality today.

Beyond communicating the vision verbally, as the leader of the company it is my responsibility to incarnate or embody the vision. I must set the example through my behavior. I must be willing to see myself as the servant of the organization. What this means is that the members of the organization must see me act out the language. In the vernacular of the 1960s, I must not only "talk the talk, but walk the walk." I can measure my success at this by asking, "Whom have I served today?"

Last year, on a Saturday afternoon, when our maintenance company came into one of our service departments to clean, I was there waiting for them in my work clothes. Obviously they were surprised. I told them that I was disappointed about the cleanliness of our dealerships, but that it would be inappropriate for me to be critical until I demonstrated how I defined "clean." I spent the evening with them cleaning.

Developing People

As Christians, we believe that each person is created in the image of God. No matter how flawed or dull the image, each of us is the repository of value beyond description, a value so great that God sent His only Son to the cross on our behalf. Consequently, there are no "ordinary people."

This means that I must work to create a business environment that affirms the dignity and worth of each individual. At the least, this means that I cannot allow the value of a person to be equated with his or her relative position within the organization. Every person has a right to be affirmed as having value that extends beyond his or her ability to produce work. Respect and dignity flow from the fact that we are created in the image of God, not that we are able to produce at a certain level.

A consequence of being made in the image of God is that we are co-creators with God in this world. We seek to bring expression to this belief. The desire to understand, to learn, to grow, and to develop are intrinsic to the very foundation of our being.

As a leader committed to exercising my authority through service, I have attempted to develop a corporate paradigm for the development of people. I have written a lengthy essay on this topic. Based on biblical values, the piece is distributed throughout the company. Now we are developing a number of seminars with learning exercises that address these key values.

"Second Chances" is the theme of our program for personal development, and that is the primary value in the paradigm. We have defined second chances as the space or freedom for failure as we strive to improve. We recognize that we will make mistakes, but we believe that this program points to the profound concept of grace. It provides the opportunity for a second chance for those who are trying to grow and improve. Without grace, there is no hope for genuine personal growth.

Building on this is the concept of reflective openness—a willingness to challenge our own ideas, to look truthfully at who we are and what we do. Reflective openness is grounded in an approach to life that is open to change and willing to learn. Central is the belief that every person has equal value and is capable of teaching us something new. It implies a deep humility before the truth that none of us has all the answers.

The apex of our paradigm for the development of people is personal development, the molding of individual competency and character. This concept implies a great deal more than simply being good at one's job. Personal competency means living an integrated life. For those in leadership, it means that we must recognize the interconnectedness of life. Each sphere of life—family, work, friends, civic, recreation—has an impact on the others. Leaders who are committed to the development of their people care about the whole person, and they model this in their own lives.

The character of leaders is a powerful force. Leaders will get the behavior they model. When you look at the behavior of the people who work for you, you are looking into a mirror and seeing your own reflection.

Finally, the development of people means caring enough about the people in the organization not only to develop their gifts, but also to hold them accountable for exercising them. If we truly believe that every person's contribution is important for the well-being of the organization, for the good of the community, then we must create a structure that promotes the growth of gifts.

Building Community

It has been said that companies will be the neighborhoods of the 1990s. Many people in our nonchurched, mobile culture will find their community life in their workplace. As relational beings created to live in community, our work life offers an opportunity for meaningful human experience.

As Christians, this provides us with an excellent opportunity to work towards creating a level of relationships that point to the kingdom of God. We believe community building experiences must be purposefully developed. We affirm the life of the community by celebrating birthdays, sponsoring company athletic teams, sending flowers, going to company-sponsored family activities, running company blood banks, participating in the United Way, cooking Christmas dinners, writing cards, holding company picnics, going to weddings, going to funerals, giving baby showers, buying graduation presents, and celebrating family days. These are all part of the community experience we try to build.

Additionally, just as we have designed a formal paradigm for the development of people, we have also created one for building community. Truth-telling is its foundation. Telling the truth means that we are relentless in our efforts to accurately describe what is really happening. We must seek to make decisions based on facts, not on opinions, rumors, or prejudices. We must have the courage to ask: What is the truth in this situation? What is the truth in this person's performance?

Truth-telling is the foundation for developing trust. Simply stated, we trust people we can believe in, and we believe in people who tell the truth. Trust develops when we know we can depend on the person beside us to do what is right.

Building trust is critical for creating an environment for teamwork. When we trust each other, we can build on each other's strengths while we honestly address our individual weaknesses. We learn to see situations through the eyes of different people. As a team, the potential of our collective intelligence far surpasses what any of us can do alone. Working together, we can create a strong sense of community that is a powerful source of meaning in people's lives.

To create this sense of community, organizational structure, leadership styles, and compensation plans must be congruent with the governing commitments of the company. These elements must reinforce one another. Our organizational structure is extremely flat. We have attempted to create an environment where management's and nonmanagement's behavior is not determined by a hierarchy. Rather, it is controlled by the shared vision and values of the organization. The authority of management is not derived from its organization chart. Instead, it flows from commitment to the vision.

As you can see, we are striving to make grace and truth the two foundational values in our company. In his Gospel, John wrote that when "the Word became flesh and made his dwelling among us [He was] full of grace and truth" (Jn. 1:14). Grace and truth were the hallmarks of the Incarnate Word, and I believe they are central to pointing people to the Risen Lord.

In my experience this emphasis upon the relational and personal dimension of organization life creates a genuine sense of purpose and meaning in the workplace for employees. Their work begins to make a positive contribution to their lives, and they make a significant contribution to the work community.

Integrating Prayer

I conclude these thoughts by addressing an extremely important issue for most marketplace Christians. *How is my service to Christ infused with the power of the Holy Spirit so that my life truly reflects the kingdom of God?*

The Christian tradition points to prayer as the answer to this question. But for those in the marketplace, praying about or for our work life feels awkward. For what exactly do I pray? More profit? A budget request approval? Guidance concerning difficult employees? A promotion?

The following format has been extremely helpful for me in integrating prayer into my work life. Because my personal vision and the corporate vision closely overlap, I make this a central feature of my prayer life. I pray that customers and employees might experience the aroma of Christ as we serve them, and that our service will be infused with the power of the Holy Spirit. I pray that we might have the discipline to look to other's needs before we look to our own. I pray for faithfulness to our mission as it relates to fulfilling our call to service. And I pray for forgiveness when we have failed to live faithfully to our calling.

Finally, I try to pray specifically for the organization in a structured manner. In the personal dimension, I pray for individual employees, their lives, their personal and professional struggles, and for them to come to Christ. At the relational dimension, I pray for us as a community where truth and grace might reign. I confess regularly my own shortcomings in this area. I also pray regularly for relationships, for reconciliations, and for the development of trust. Regarding the technological or systems dimension, I pray for wisdom concerning how to integrate it into the human community, how to let it assist us in fulfilling our vision of service. In the economic dimension, I pray for the profits we need to sustain our commitment to our mission, vision, and core values.

I offer these thoughts, not because I have any significant spiritual insight, but because I am striving to know what it means to experience the kingdom of God in daily life. I hope these thoughts stimulate you to reflect upon what it means to live faithfully for Christ in your specific place. And I pray that the eyes of your heart might be opened to see the world and feel the world with the eyes and heart of Jesus Christ.

Questions for Discussion

Vocational Integration: Living Faithfully for Christ

1. Our responsibility is to discover what our calling means in the particular concrete place where God's sovereignty has placed us. Pursuing this is critical for developing a conscious sense of being aligned
   with the will of God. One exercise to help discover this is to develop
   your own set of Governing Commitments. This involves examining
   the issues of Mission (your purpose in the workplace), Vision (how
   your gifts and motivated abilities will be exercised in service to Christ
   (inside and outside the organization), and Values (what qualities will
   characterize your life in the marketplace). This exercise should be
   conducted with much prayer and in consultation with those who know
   you well.

2. Reflect on the following biblical words: faith, hope, love, grace,
   truth. These words are clear signposts to the Kingdom of God. How
   can you embody and articulate them in your workplace so that others
   might taste of the Kingdom?

3. Living faithfully for Christ means experiencing systemically salvation, sanctification, and service. Does the Christian community where
   you fellowship encourage the integration of these into daily life?

4. Learning how to pray about your life in the marketplace means beginning to think about the time you spend there as a central place of
   ministry (service). Consider praying for everyone you come in contact with on a daily basis that your life might point to the kingdom
   of God. Pray for opportunities where you can concretely demonstrate
   the love of Jesus that transforms lives.

5. Our work itself can be a "spiritual sacrifice" where we exercise obedience to Christ. Consider offering each act you do during the day

to the "glory of God." Even the most mundane work then becomes pregnant with eternal significance.

6. Reflect on the primary values you experience at work in your organi zation. What is the belief structure concerning the nature of reality, the source of meaning, the purpose of work, the value of people that is providing the foundation for the values that are lived out in your organization. Can you infuse your organization with biblical founda tion as you seek to build a community of people striving together for a common purpose?

VII.

Reflecting Christ in the Banking Industry:
The Manager as Prophet, Priest, and King

Sandra Herron

During Israel's journey through the wilderness, the Lord speaks to Moses: "Send out for yourself men so that they may spy out the land of Canaan, which I am going to give to the sons of Israel" (Num. 13:2). So Moses dispatches twelve scouts to explore the promised land. After forty days the spies return to report on their findings. They agree on the facts: The land flows with milk and honey (suggesting extreme fertility), but its occupants are big and powerful, and the cities are well fortified. However, the scouts are seriously divided on what to do next. Ten of them can see only the strength of their adversaries and recommend that the Israelites abort their trip. Caleb and Joshua disagree, and Caleb has the courage to speak out: "We should by all means go up and take possession of it, for we shall surely overcome it" (Num. 13:30). These two faithful men did not underestimate the power of the Lord.

It is into this land of giants that God has called us to join Him in His continuing work of creation, revelation, and redemption. The work of God goes forth when Christian men and women become God's partners in bringing new life to a broken world. While the giants often may appear too strong to conquer, God promises His presence and power and gives us a vision of His plan.

In this chapter I will explore God's call to men and women to participate in the ongoing work of Christ in their respective workplaces. In addition, I will examine the threefold office of Christ as one model that can help us understand how a manager may manifest Christ's presence in the workplace. Finally, I will propose some reasons why greater numbers of men and women do not view their work as advancing the kingdom of God.

Sent Into the World

In Christ, God was reconciling the world to Himself, and we have been entrusted with the message of reconciliation (II Cor. 5:19). Jesus' prayer for the disciples helps us understand the nature of our call: "My prayer is not that you take them out of the world but that you protect them from the evil one . . . As you sent me into the world, I have sent them into the world" (Jn. 17:15, 18). The whole world is the object of God's saving work, and we are co-workers with God (I Cor. 3:9) to accomplish this redemptive act.

Thus, the marketplace is not a place to be avoided; rather, it is our assignment! As Christ's disciples, we are called into secular institutions to help lead them into better performance for the public good. Our mission is in the world, where we serve as partners with Christ in building the kingdom—in government, in corporations, in the entertainment industry, in educational institutions, in our inner cities, in foreign lands, even in our churches. Wherever our hearts echo with the pain of brokenness and sin, God can use us to bring healing and reconciliation to a groaning creation.

Yet we do not pursue our own vision; rather, we have been "arrested by a higher loyalty and gripped by a mighty cause."[1] The Holy Spirit inspires us to invest our desires, motivations, and gifts for God's purposes. Insofar as we are people who have been transformed by the Gospel, God in Christ can work through us to lead change in our culture and institutions. As we serve faithfully, do justice, and establish righteousness, we bear witness to Jesus Christ and bring the Gospel to all people and structures and patterns of society.

Our work becomes our grateful response to what God has done and the arena in which our faith is worked out for the good of the world. Perhaps it is easier to view work as advancing the kingdom of God when we work for a church, religious organization, or missionary group. But if God desires that the entire creation be redeemed, then the importance of secular work cannot be ignored. Consider these words from the theologian Frederick Buechner:

> The kind of work God usually calls you to is the kind of work (a) that you need most to do and (b) that the world most needs to have done . . . The place God calls you to is the place where your deep gladness and the world's deep hunger meet.[2]

When we prayerfully consider our own talents and gifts in light of the
world and its needs, God can help us to answer the cries of His world.

But what does it look like to manifest Jesus Christ in the workplace
and to be the people of God at work in the world? What difference does
a relationship with Jesus Christ make in our daily work? How does the
Gospel speak to our workplace priorities and frustrations? How can we
summon the courage each day to enter a land full of giants with the confidence of Caleb? By examining the work of Christ, we can better understand how our work can be consistent with God's intentions for the
world.

The Work of Christ

Theologically, *the work of Christ* refers to Jesus Christ's saving work as
portrayed through three distinct offices or roles: prophet, priest, and
king. In His role as prophet, Jesus reveals God's saving purposes so that
we might know the way of forgiveness that God has provided for us.
Jesus does not speak on His own initiative, but brings the Father's message (Jn. 12:49) and proclaims it to the people (Mt. 4:17). Christ also
foretells or predicts future events (Mt. 24-25).

In His work as king, Christ restores His wandering sheep to their
right path. He calls out of the world a people for Himself (Jn. 16:27),
gives them a specific assignment (Mt. 28:19-20), and provides them with
varieties of gifts, ministries, and workings so that God's purposes might
be accomplished (I Cor. 12:4ff). His grace and power are sufficient (II
Cor. 12:9) to support us in temptation and suffering, and He overcomes
all enemies (I Cor. 15:25). He deals out "retribution to those who do not
know God and to those who do not obey the gospel of our Lord Jesus"
(II Th. 1:8) and orders all things to bring glory to God (Rom. 8:28).

In His role as priest, Jesus brings forgiveness and redemption. He
offers Himself up to God as the "once for all" sacrifice (Heb. 10:10) so
that we might be reconciled to God. He makes continual intercession for
those who draw near to God through Him (Heb. 7:25).

Since Christ continues His ministry through us, our ministry can
also be characterized by this threefold office. I find this model valuable
in helping me discern ways in which my work is consistent with God's
continuing work of revelation. As Robert Benne writes:

To make a comfortable living, to find work fulfilling, to perform a useful service to others, and to see all of this as participation in the loving intentions of God lights up the soul.[3]

In what follows, I will expand on the threefold office as it relates to my own work as a Christian manager. While my language, illustrations, and questions are shaped by my recent roles as a bank vice president and service company department head, I offer them with the hope of stimulating reflection on how Christ may be made known through your own work.

The Manager as Prophet

The Greek word *prophetes* means "one who speaks for a god and interprets his will to man."[4] Biblical prophets were certain that God had spoken to them and that they were called to speak God's message.[5] The prophet:

> . . . is deeply involved in the life and death of his own nation. He speaks about the king and his idolatrous practices, prophets who say what they are paid to say, priests who fail to instruct the people in Yahweh's law, merchants who use false balances, judges who favor the rich and give no justice to the poor, greedy women who drive their husbands to evil practices so they can bask in luxury . . . Prophecy is not simply God's message to the present situation, but is intended primarily to show how that situation fits into his plan, how he will use it to judge and refine or comfort and encourage his people. Prophecy is God's message to the present in light of his ongoing redemptive purpose.[6]

First, then, prophecy is speaking the right word at the right time. Prophets bring a word from the Lord to a particular place and in a particular manner. If we are to continue Christ's prophetic ministry in the workplace, we must be willing to challenge the *status quo* and envision a new reality that brings us closer to the values of the kingdom. In a competitive, dog-eat-dog marketplace, many will find this a difficult role to fulfill. Yet, when we question prevailing norms we most clearly see how Christ's work continues today in the workplace.

Let me give an example. In banking, as in many industries, there is a concept referred to as *differentiated service strategies*. In plain English, this means that different customers receive different levels of service. A bank's most profitable customers might be assigned a personal banking representative, be shown to a special (shorter) branch line, and be given special gifts or privileges throughout the year. Yet admonitions about the sin of partiality (Jas. 2:7) cause me to question this generally accepted practice. Is preferential treatment for special groups of customers legitimate? If so, when does such treatment become unfairly discriminatory to others?

When I worked in the payroll industry, one of our competitors had a policy whereby set-up charges could be negotiated by the customer and salesperson. As a result, a customer with good negotiating skills might have paid nothing up-front, while another customer might have paid as much as $1,200. To further complicate the process, the salesperson received fifty percent of the negotiated set-up charges, so there was a great incentive to collect as high a fee as possible. This practice of charging different prices to different customers for the same product or service is common in sales organizations, but few sales managers ever ask whether such a strategy is consistent with God's intentions and standards.

For the manager who prayerfully asks for the wisdom to raise the right issues, the questions are endless. How do I respond to a colleague who insists that there is no morality in pricing? How can I show special consideration for unique personal circumstances and still treat people fairly and impartially? Is shopping the competition an acceptable means of gathering market intelligence so that we might compete more aggressively?

When we raise these types of concerns, we are exercising a prophetic role. Unfortunately, a corporate prophet who questions existing policies and practices is rarely well received. Strong support and encouragement from a caring Christian community is critical for anyone who regularly finds himself or herself in such a role.

A second and critical component of the prophetic office is the ability to envision a new reality, for "where there is no vision the people perish" (Pr. 29:18). I have found managers and co-workers much more receptive if, after questioning a routine procedure, I propose a creative alternative that can be easily integrated within our operation. So, when I criticize an incentive program, I also suggest a new plan that encourages teamwork and provides for a more equitable distribution of rewards.

This is where Christians can have a profound impact on the market-place. The ability to see beyond what *is* and offer a dream of what *might be* is a gift. Former President George Bush was criticized for not having "the vision thing." Yet most of us are so enslaved by time and economic pressures that we are unable or unwilling to step back and view things from a fresh perspective. There is a risk associated with putting on new glasses. The "way we have always done it" is familiar and safe, while the new way may be unknown and frightening.

The prophetic imperative also demands that we name the Name. As we fight for change, we have opportunities to share the Gospel in ways that are sensible and appropriate for the circumstances. For example, when someone compliments the way in which I write performance reviews, I explain why it is so important to be honest with people, to help them understand their unique giftedness, and to enable them to become all they can be.

As a manager, I play a key role in helping to define my company's relationships with our employees, our customers, and the larger society. I have plenty of opportunities to integrate kingdom values into the corporate culture. My company is like most others. People spend a lot of time looking after their own psychological needs, delivering monologues on their opinions, guarding their turf, comparing their progress to that of others, trying to elevate their own status, and criticizing those who are different. In contrast, we are called to foster dialogue, affirm each other, value and promote diversity and dissenting voices, celebrate unity, appreciate potential, and encourage development. The prophet's role is to help people and organizations discover all that God intends for us to become.

The Manager as King

The vision of the prophet becomes reality through the kingly, or administrative, ministry. In ancient Israel, the king was viewed as God's representative charged with enforcing and embodying the covenant. Ideally, at least, he was a servant of the people. The king's primary responsibilities were to maintain peace within the kingdom by governing effectively and justly and to protect his subjects from outside attack. If such an attack should occur, the king was prepared to oppose the enemy and subdue him.

Christ our King rules over all people and all creation. We can participate in that kingly ministry through faithful stewardship of God's *created* order. In my work, good stewardship has to do with managing physical resources—such as money, facilities, and technology—as well as ensuring that the gifts and talents of my employees are effectively utilized. That requires, among other things, that I be conservative in my budgeting and frugal in spending company money. I look for ways to avoid waste, such as making sure that machines and lights are turned off at night, reducing paperwork, and eliminating unnecessary reports. Our office participates in paper and aluminum recycling, and uses technology to operate more efficiently and improve the quality of our work.

But the clearest link between my work and the kingly ministry of Jesus Christ is in my role as a manager of human resources. God has gifted each person with different capacities, ministries, and competencies (I Cor. 12:4ff), and when we come together as a body to work out the plan of God, we bring certain talents and abilities. This requires great care in allowing each team member the opportunity to exercise his or her unique gifts. Recruitment must be thoughtful and assignments must be carefully divided.

The Bible contains some wonderful models of kingly (and queenly) ministry. For example, Nehemiah's strong leadership skills made it possible for God's purposes to be accomplished. When Nehemiah called upon the people of Jerusalem to rebuild the walls, he made sure everyone knew the goal and was committed to the work. Nehemiah's example helps us understand that the king's ability to make things happen is linked to his ability to build a sense of community.

Jesus Christ was the King of Kings, yet He took on the nature of a servant to reveal the love of God and bring us into right relationship with our Creator. The kingdom of God is manifested in the workplace when the *king* takes on the nature of a *servant*, acting as a resource and enabler —and sometimes even as a protector from "enemy attacks" within the organization.

The Manager as Priest

In the Old Testament, priests were responsible for the conduct of worship, for the tabernacle or temple, and for all the sacrifices and festivals that pertained to religious life. Through atonement and intercession, the priests restored fellowship between a holy God and the sinful people. Today, the crucified and risen Christ continually performs the work of a priest on our behalf.

We continue Christ's priestly ministry in the workplace when we point to His redemptive work and bear witness to His kingdom. When we care for others, celebrate with them, and try to serve as a model for them, we are fulfilling a priestly, or pastoral, office.

In most cases, business organizations are not easy places in which to exercise a priestly role. Some might argue that care, compassion, and love are not compatible with the drive for bottom-line results. Yet, as consumer expectations continue to increase, many companies are placing a greater emphasis on customer service. How ironic that customer satisfaction primarily depends upon caring and compassion, and is, in essence, love in action! When we ask our satisfied customers what they like about doing business with us, they say things like, "She really cared about me as a person," or "He made me feel like I was important and valuable." Our customers want to be treated as individuals and work with caring and responsive employees. And since, as customer service guru Karl Albrecht says, "The way your employees feel is ultimately the way your customers will feel,"[7] we must begin with the employees who serve those customers.

Care and compassion can—and must—be integrated with our drive for profitability. The entire management process must begin with the heart, not just because it is good business, but because it is right and consistent with God's intentions. As a manager, I try to be loving and supportive, rather than harsh or disinterested. I let employees know that I care about them as valuable and unique individuals because of who they are, not just what they do and contribute to our department. Even developing a training program to help our employees deal more effectively with irate customers and service problems could be considered a form of caring.[8]

We can call attention to God's presence in the workplace through acts of celebration. Our department places a high value on celebration, both for personal and professional achievements. We remember birthdays and rejoice in family additions. We celebrate new programs, successful programs, and completed programs. Once we even celebrated the "passing away" of a burdensome assignment to another area of the organization! It seems to me that such rituals can somehow help us see linkages between God's reconciling action and everyday events in the workplace.

Our personal behavior can serve as a testimony to what God in Christ has done for us and to the presence of God in our lives. As part of the new creation in Christ, we can offer the hope of change to others who may be stuck or struggling. To encourage a trainee who finds it difficult to work with a particular manager, I can recount similar personal problems and outline the attitudes and behaviors I found helpful. To comfort an employee struggling with perfectionism and ambition, I can offer guidance gained from my own continuing battles.

Although I feel called to the mission field of American business, occasionally I question whether and how my work is really contributing to the building of the kingdom of God. At these moments, God sometimes gives me a glimpse of His vision; I call these "kingdom breakthroughs."

About a year ago I was given responsibility for a new department and several additional employees. My predecessor in the job did not encourage employee participation, and I knew my first challenge would be to unleash the creativity of the staff and get them involved in setting our new direction and priorities. As I talked with one employee (whom I'll call Mary), I was painfully aware of how hard it was for her to offer any ideas. Finally, with great enthusiasm and dramatic gestures, I said, "Now, Mary, I want you to reach deep down inside. You're a very talented woman. If you had no time or financial constraints, what would you really like to do?" After a minute, she suggested a wonderful new program. I praised her creativity and asked for another proposal. Soon the ideas were flowing like a waterfall! As we concluded our meeting, she looked at me with great emotion and said, "No one has ever asked for my ideas before."

Missing Connections

Why do so few Christians make any connection between Sunday worship and Monday work? Many of us have never heard anyone speak of a connection between faith and work, particularly in a sermon. Even after years of intense theological study, many clergy find themselves ill-prepared to tackle the real issues that confront ordinary people, particularly in the realm of vocational concerns and dilemmas.

Consider these thoughts from a Japanese missionary:

> On the way to the country church, I never fail to see a herd of water buffaloes grazing in the muddy paddy field. This sight is an inspiring moment for me. Why? Because it reminds me that the people to whom I am to bring the Gospel of Christ spend most of their time with these water buffaloes in the rice field. The water buffaloes . . . remind me to discard all abstract ideas, and to use exclusively objects that are immediately tangible . . . . Then I ask myself, "Is this introduction understandable and realistic in terms of *their* daily experiences? Is this message digestible and nutritious to *their* ethical and theological needs?"[9]

When we seek to communicate the Gospel message, we must begin where the people are, then call God into these real human situations. That means employing language and symbols that connect with common life, penetrate into areas of ignorance, and provoke reflection and decision.

There are some who discern vague connections between faith and work. Yet many feel they lack the confidence and competence to make a difference in the workplace. They complain that they have too little time to be adequately equipped for the job and point out that there are too few resources to help them even if they found the time. Our churches, for the most part, remain preoccupied with programs and structures. "Training the laity" too often means equipping nonordained Christians for the work of the church gathered, rather than preparing us to be the church in the world. Rarely is work done outside the church recognized as valid ministry.

Our churches must join men and women where they are, affirm as ministry what their members are doing, and help us identify and reflect upon those connections between faith and daily work. The church gathered should equip us, empower us, send us, and hold us accountable for our unique ministries in the world. The church then can provide a place to gather and celebrate, be recognized and equipped, become empowered and sent back again. There should be a rhythm of withdrawal from and return to the world, with the church acting not as an oasis, but more like a dispatch operation. The Christian comes to the altar to be renewed by Christ and returns to the world to do Christ's work.

Though we may feel overwhelmed by this call and make excuses that we are inadequate for the task, like Moses, God can and will use us—wherever we work, live, and play—if only we will allow it. Perhaps this is the biggest obstacle of all. Are we really ready for Christ to be Lord over all areas of our lives and to face the implications for our work? Are we willing to deal with the inevitable conflict of values that occurs when we seek to apply biblical principles to our Monday through Friday agendas? Are we prepared to face ridicule and exploitation as we fulfill prophetic, priestly, and kingly roles in our institutions?

We know that the struggle between the old and new will continue until God brings about the fulfillment of His kingdom. We know that every day we will not do all the good we can do. We are constantly reminded that, although we are saved by faith, we are yet sinners. Still, the Holy Spirit uses our response of faith for the good of the world, and we work to help usher forth the kingdom of God.

In C. S. Lewis' *The Chronicles of Narnia,* we read of a question that reminds us of one we must all be ready to answer:

> "Son of Adam," said Aslan. "Are you ready to undo the wrong that you have done to my sweet country of Narnia on the very day of its birth?"
>
> "Well, I don't see what I can do," said Digory. "You see, the Queen ran away and —"
>
> "I asked, are you ready?" said the Lion.[10]

As men and women of God, we are called to be kingdom-builders, in the workplace and in every corner of the world. Although we may find ourselves in uncharted and unknown lands, we know that angels fight on our side and rejoice in our progress. And as we set out to conquer these new frontiers, we need each other to discover what it means to be part of the Body of Christ in these places, so that we may press forward to reclaim every single square inch of creation for the glory of God.

Notes

1. R. Paul Stevens and Gerry Schoberg, *Satisfying Work: Christian Living from Nine to Five* (Wheaton, IL: Harold Shaw Publishers, 1989), 55.

2. Frederick Buechner, *Wishful Thinking: A Theological ABC* (New York: Harper and Row, 1973), 95.

3. Robert Benne, *Ordinary Saints, Introduction to the Christian Life* (Philadelphia: Fortress Press, 1988), 165.

4. H.G. Liddell and R. Scott, *A Greek-English Lexicon,* ed. H.S. Jones, 9th ed. (New York: 1940), 2:1540a.

5. For further study, read the call narratives in Is. 6:1-13; Jer. 1:4-10; Ezek. 1:1-3; Hos. 1:2-9 and 8:1-5; Am. 3:1-8 and 7:12-15.

6. William Sanford LaSor, David Allan Hubbard, Frederic Wm. Bush, *Old Testament Survey: The Message, Form and Background of the Old Testament* (Grand Rapids, MI: William B. Eerdmans Publishing Company, 1982), 305.

7. Karl Albrecht, *The Only Thing That Matters* (New York: Harper Collins Publishers, 1992), 93.

8. See generally on this, James A. Autry, *Love and Profit: The Art of Caring Leadership* (New York: Morrow and Co., 1991).

9. Kosuke Koyama, *Water Buffalo Theology* (Maryknoll, New York: Orbis Books, 1974), vii-viii.

10. C. S. Lewis, *The Magician's Nephew* (New York: Macmillan, 1955), 141.

Questions for Discussion

1. Are you able to view your work as advancing the kingdom of God? In what ways do you, or could you, express the conviction that you are working for God?

2. How can the threefold office of Christ model help you uncover new ways of continuing Christ's ministry in your workplace?

3. What conflicts do you see between biblical principles and your workplace priorities?

4. Have you ever played the role of prophet in your workplace by challenging a policy that seemed inconsistent with kingdom values? With whom did you come into conflict?

5. Who are the most significant people in your life? Do you have role models from whom you can learn about changing your workplace to the glory of God?

VIII.
The Teacher as Revealer and Role Model: Education as a Reflection of the Incarnation

Steve Garber

Recently I had a conversation with a young man who had just spent four years in London as a study assistant under John Stott.[1] After praying, studying, and working with this respected theologian and pastor, this young man had come to Washington to pursue his calling in the next season of his life. He sought to know the Word and the world, to be a student of Scripture and a student of the society, much like Stott. The marks of the teacher's vision and vocation were plainly revealed in the heart and mind of his apprentice.

And that, simply said, is how it should be.

Somewhere deeply woven into the fabric of Stott's life is a thread that connects him to one of the best-loved stories of teachers and their students, Thomas Hughes' *Tom Brown's School Days*. Set in the Rugby School in nineteenth-century England—Stott's school a century later—it is a tale of teaching at its truest. Like all other boys of his social class, Tom was sent off for the years of preparation required for entrance to an Oxbridge education. He experienced all the loneliness and fears that are common to little boys, whichever rung they occupy on the social ladder. Tom spent eight years at Rugby, growing from a young boy to a young man.

Central to the story, and to Tom's own character formation, is the school's headmaster, Dr. Arnold. A lover of God and a lover of learning, he is a man whose moral vision gives shape and substance to schooling at Rugby. In his first week at school, Tom joined three hundred other boys for Sunday prayers, which were led by Dr. Arnold.

> The tall gallant form, the kindling eye, the voice, now soft as the
> low notes of a flute, now clear and stirring as the call of the light

infantry bugle, of him who stood there Sunday after Sunday, witnessing and pleading for his Lord, the King of righteousness and
love and glory, with whose spirit he was filled, and in whose power
he spoke.[2]

Through the eyes and ears of Tom, we experience the wonder of
worship in the Rugby chapel. The stained-glass silence, the shadow-light
of a hundred candles, the first rumblings of the organ—it is as if we are
seated with Tom, fearfully and expectantly listening to Dr. Arnold call
his students to a full-bodied faith.

Hughes' account is historical fiction. And yet there was a Dr.
Arnold, and there is a Rugby School, and John Stott, like the Tom
Browns before him, did grow from boyhood to manhood there. What
Hughes captured in his portrait of Dr. Arnold was a man whose earnest-
ness for God made his students want to be like him.

It would be more romance than reality to argue that the Rugby
School was a bastion of godliness and good learning. Rather, my point is
this: Stott stands in a long line of Anglican leaders whose pastoral and
theological vision has been deeply wrought by a love for God and a love
for learning. There are men and women all over the world who have
heard and read Stott, and who have taken that passion for *godly learning*
into a variety of vocations. These people have remembered the model of
a man who earnestly taught them how to live in the world under the
Word—thinking carefully and caring deeply.

But what is true of Stott and his students—those who have had the
privilege of face-to-face tutorials and those who have heard or read him
from afar—is true for the truest teaching always and everywhere. In this
chapter I will explore the two themes, as a way of understanding the
vocation of teacher and the meaning of teaching. The first is that God
Himself, incarnate in Jesus Christ, is the master teacher. The second is
that the American Studies Program, in its incarnational approach to
teaching, is a creative response to the challenges of the modern world in
the area of education.

REVELATION AND RESPONSE:
Theological Reflection on Teaching

For people who follow Jesus as Lord, whose discipleship is shaped by the Scriptures, two basic patterns emerge as we reflect on the Bible's teaching about teaching: God reveals Himself to people who have the ability to respond, and their response is integrally dependent upon their knowledge of God.

God Reveals Himself to Responsible People

From Adam to Abraham, from Moses to Malachi, from Jesus to John, the primary revelation in the Scriptures is of God himself. From the first words of Genesis, where God reveals that the heavens and the earth are His creation, to His gracious provision of Eve to Adam, to His prophetic pronouncement of cosmic conflict between the seed of the woman and the seed of the serpent, on through His choice of a family—Abraham, Isaac, Jacob—to be the carrier of His promises into history, we see revealed on the pages of Genesis the God of creation, providence, and redemption. And we see it revealed because God chooses to reveal it. God wants us to know Him.

As this account of God's work in history is unfolded, we see that knowing His nature and character provides a context for hearing God's Law. But it is in this revelation of the Law that we come to know God even more fully. Through the Torah inscribed on stone tablets, God is revealed as the one who established a universe where there is true good and true evil, and where choices have consequences.

Somehow written deeply into the reality of God's sovereign care and mercy for His creation is also the God who reveals the divine nature to those with ears to hear. These are deep waters, but the Bible teaches quite plainly that while God is completely sovereign, human beings are completely responsible. This has enormous implications for teachers. Our vocation is always within that biblical tension as those fundamental truths frame our life in the universe.

God reveals Himself in history and the Law, calling out a people from Abraham's seed and providentially placing them at the center of the civilizations. Implicit in that call was the expectation of responsibility, namely, an ability to respond. From the first Adam and Eve, God created humans with the moral ability to respond. And from the beginning, most did not respond. Nine generations later, Noah alone was "a righteous man, blameless among the people of his time" (Gen. 6:9).[3] And as the generations pass, the people of Israel, chosen to know God, more often than not, chose not to follow God.

We need to see two realities here. One is that God so loved the world that in His sovereign mercy He provided a way of redemption; from Genesis to Revelation, it is always "the blood of the lamb" that takes away the sin of the world. But it is in that saving work that God is most profoundly known; justice and mercy meet in God's redemptive action. The "Holy, Holy, Holy" God of Isaiah's vision (Is. 9) is "compassionate and gracious, slow to anger, abounding in love" (Ps. 103:8). The second reality is that God's revelation requires, by implication, a response. We are responsible. Our choices are real and they have consequences that ripple on through history. These two realities are held together throughout the Bible, and they are critical for us as we reflect theologically on the vocation of teacher.

These grand biblical themes come as amazing grace in the Incarnation. The long-awaited promise of Genesis 3:15 is brought into being in the person and work of Christ. He is God in the flesh. Because that is true, Jesus reveals Himself as the Promised One of Isaiah's prophecy (Lk. 4:13-30) who expects a response (Lk. 5:1-11). If the pages of the gospels show anything plainly, it is that Jesus is "the Word made flesh" who has come from the Father "full of grace and truth" (Jn. 1:14), and that Jesus assumes that some will have "ears to hear" (Mt. 13:1-9). So, God wants to be known so much that He sends His Son to live for awhile among us, but this divine revelation assumes a moral ability to respond. The teaching of Jesus always reflects these two realities.

But the teaching of Jesus only makes sense if we understand the world view of Jesus, particularly the Hebrew understanding of knowledge. Jesus the son of Mary, stepson of Joseph, was trained to think like a Jew. For Jesus the Jew, at one and the same time the Son of David and the Son of the Most High God, knowledge implied responsibility. *Knowing meant doing.*

I find in my teaching, whether with my children or with my students, that it is very hard to connect with those Hebrew roots. We live in a world where knowing does not mean doing, where knowledge implies everything but responsibility. "Yes, I know that *theoretically*, but *practically* speaking . . ." and we walk off in the other direction, relieving ourselves of any responsibility for our knowledge.

For the Hebrews, knowing implied doing. If you didn't do, then you didn't know: *knowledge of* means *responsibility to*, means *care for*.[4] This dynamic understanding of knowledge is a long way from our modern dispassionate approach to it. If knowing means caring, then knowing means caring for God (Dt. 4:39-40). It means caring for other human beings (Pr. 29:7), and it means caring for creation (Pr. 12:10).

So, what have we learned about teaching? As God reveals, so God draws people to himself; God has created a moral universe where knowledge implies responsibility. Again, it is that tension that decisively determines the dynamics of teaching. And we have seen that Jesus, as God Incarnate, models for us a kind of teaching that is deeply rooted in those two realities.

Jesus as the Teacher of Teachers

We need to learn from Jesus. Yes, of course there are implications for everyone who follows Him—whether butcher, baker, or candle-stick-maker—but there are particular implications for those of us who teach. The people of His time saw Him as a teacher, and more often than not called Him "Rabbi." There is something in His vocation that is for us *as teachers*.

As I have studied the life of Jesus with an eye to understanding His teaching, three principles have become clear: 1) people learn by seeing the truth done, 2) people learn by doing the truth, and 3) people learn by hearing the truth taught with integrity. In and through all of this is a vision of discipleship that is understood as apprenticeship; literally, *apprentice* is the deepest root of the word *disciple*.

Throughout the gospels we hear Jesus saying, "Come, follow me." In Mark's account, Jesus announces the presence of His kingdom, (1:15) and then invites particular people to come be with Him. Woven into the story is the thread of His self-revelation; for example, the man possessed with an evil spirit who says, "I know who you are—the Holy One of God!" or His first encounter with the teachers of the law in the next chapter, where His identity is the central issue, "Who can forgive sins but

God alone?" (2:1-12). As Jesus draws together the twelve, He wants His disciples to learn from Him by watching Him live, by sleeping where He sleeps, and by sharing meals with Him. As He feeds thousands, as He heals little girls, as He talks with prostitutes, He wants His apprentices to be with Him. Why? Because people learn by seeing the truth done.

We don't know how long it took, but after months of watching Jesus, the twelve are finally "pushed out of the nest" (Mk. 6:7-30). Jesus gives them the opportunity to learn by doing. And so He sent them out, two by two, to minister by teaching and healing—as they had seen Him do. Some time later, they came home and reported to Jesus "all they had done and taught." It is as if Jesus said to them, "Now you do it" and then called them together, asking "Now how did you do?" He understood, as the Master Teacher, that people learn by doing the truth.

Finally, Jesus teaches us that people learn by hearing the truth taught with integrity. Painfully, one of the most poignant contrasts in the gospels is between the teachers of the law and Jesus. At so many points, the Pharisees were hypocrites. They did not practice what they preached. With righteous anger, Jesus explains:

> Isaiah was right when he prophesied about you hypocrites; as it is written: "These people honor me with their lips, but their hearts are far from me. They worship me in vain; their teachings are but rules taught by men."

Actually, the gospels tell few stories of people who responded to the integrity of Jesus' teaching. Although Zaccheus did. His interest in the Gospel and his subsequent repentance was in direct response to the integrity of Jesus' life and teaching. But more often than not, people just didn't get it. And most sadly of all, his disciples were chief among those who reacted this way.

How was that possible? Again, we remember those two realities: revelation and response. Jesus lived on earth so people could know Him, but at the same time His revelation comes to those who have eyes to see and hearts to understand. In the New Testament, to *understand* (Mt. 13:23) means to "see the implications for one's life." That happened in a decisive way when the Spirit of truth came among them, opening the eyes of their hearts to the integrity of Jesus' words and deeds. God is completely sovereign, and human beings are completely responsible.

Those truths shape our existence as human beings; we live and move within them.

Living in that tension nurtured a moral vision in those apprentices that changed the world. "Come, follow me" meant shipwreck, beatings, prison, and for some, following Jesus to the cross. But that was implicit in their understanding of discipleship because they had been taught by a teacher who understood that people learn by seeing the truth done, by doing the truth, and by hearing the truth taught with integrity. There is deep wisdom here as we reflect on the incarnational nature of the truest learning.

Linking Life with Learning:
The Example of the American Studies Program

I still remember the tears. We had just finished an afternoon examining the relevance of the kingdom of God for "the public square," when a thoughtful undergraduate came up to me and asked: "But how can this possibly apply to where I work?" And he cried. As we talked it became plain that he was trying desperately to straddle two universes: how could he integrate his personal Christian beliefs and the public world of a major Washington think tank where no one seemed to care at all about the kingdom of God?

In different ways that scene plays itself out every semester in the American Studies Program. Located on Capitol Hill, we offer an inter-disciplinary educational experience for undergraduates who come to us with two factors in common: they have some kind of concern for the larger world, and they are willing to take on the adventure of a semester away from the comfort of their own campus. Students come from all over the U.S. and Canada, forty each term, to live and learn in the nation's capital. The students spend half of their time in class, a graduate seminar-style setting; and half of their time in internships located all over the city, from the Senate to the Smithsonian, the Justice Department to court-appointed legal care for the poor, the National Endowment for the Arts to the Foundation for International Dispute Resolution.

The heartbeat of the program is the same as it was when it was envisioned by John Dellenback in the mid-1970s. He had become the Peace Corps director after having served as a congressman from Oregon, and from his own years of public service thought that there ought to be a more effective way of giving Christian students a vision for responsible public involvement. Seventeen years and 1,200 students later, we are still working away at that. The American Studies Program offers a unique vantage point on the challenges written into the vocation of teacher in the twentieth century. Both the curriculum and location of the program make it a wonderful classroom for working away at the answers; there also is a deep commitment to incarnational education. That commitment is the heart and soul of why we do what we do.

What was happening with my student? His question was not superficial, and therefore required a thoughtful answer. If what we teach is not meaningful outside the classroom, what is the point anyway? This young man was raising a question that cuts to the heart of our efforts to prepare our students to live in the world. If we are to teach—to educate for responsible action—as Nicholas Wolterstorff calls it, in a way that gives our students the intellectual and personal maturity they need to live in the world and yet not be of the world, we need to understand the world.[5]

The tears of my student caused me to reflect soberly on what and how I was teaching. I asked myself: What is causing the frustration? I knew that he had been brought up in a family that loved God and prized learning; in fact he had the benefit of having spent many years overseas. I knew him well enough to know that he saw himself as a sincere follower of Christ, whose creed was consciously informed by historic orthodoxy. But I knew also that his internship experience was his first serious engagement of the modern world. Taken all together, he cried, as he wondered, "How do I make sense of it all?"

That question—how do I make sense of it all, personally and publicly?—is at the heart of our program. Explicitly, it is the first and the last question that we ask our students to answer. Because it is a deeply human question, it deserves our best energies; we address it head-on.

As we have labored together as faculty to develop a curriculum that is true to our founding vision and responsive to the changing cultural climate, we have put together an interdisciplinary semester of study that pivots on the day-by-day interaction between life and learning. Through it all we pursue that question, allowing tears of sadness as well as tears of joy to inform our understanding of education.

We believe in God the Father . . . and therefore in coherence and meaning. So, we explain that our efforts here are intentionally interdisciplinary. Though located only a few blocks from the Capitol, it is *not* a political science program. We study politics—in fact the substance of our semester is spent on examining current policy debates—but we also study theology, philosophy, economics, international development, literature, and cultural anthropology.

Typically that is a surprise for our students, sometimes even a shock. One of the consequences of industrialization is specialization, and nowhere is that seen so keenly as in higher education, even in the liberal arts colleges from which we draw most of our students. They come to us expecting to receive their education in discrete compartments: politics is politics and theology is theology. The sad reality is that, typically, the chief point of resistance each semester is that we ask our students to take the Bible and theological reflection seriously.

This past semester a student arrived, and early on it looked like we had made a mistake in accepting him. He was a math major who wanted an internship in architecture and seemed to have no interest in politics. How did he get through our application process, we wondered? But his first paper indicated that he was willing to think. At his midterm evaluation, when I visited him at the architecture firm, he again impressed me as someone who thought quite deeply and who was willing to re-examine his working assumptions about the meaning of his education and his future vocation. His journal evidenced a consistent concern to probe his foundational commitments. He was obviously reading the course texts carefully, listening in class, and trying to see it all in relation to the issues he was exploring in his internship.

One of the last essays we give students is by Stanley Hauerwas, the Duke University ethicist, in which he examines the autobiography of Albert Speer, Hitler's architect.[6] Sadly and tragically, Speer is a pristine example of the modern person whose professional identity becomes idolatrous, who becomes a "company man" to an extent that blinds him to other commitments and responsibilities. For example, he had no interest in the politics of Nazism; he only wanted to be an architect, "to build buildings which would last a millennium." You can imagine the effect of this essay on our young student. He wrote:

Reading the Hauerwas article on Speer's biography was a rather rude awakening to me. Speer's problem, it is said, could be traced back to his philosophy on life. . . "I am an architect, I'm not interested in politics." If one were to go back and look at my application

for this program one would read almost word for word, this very
sentiment. . . . Now I see that I cannot merely concentrate on architecture, but I must remain aware of the state of the world around me
. . . . So I find myself, for the first time in a long time, enlarging my
teleos, making room for political awareness so as to avoid becoming
pulled into deception.

One of the disciplines that we maintain as a faculty is eating meals
with our students. It is written into our expectations, both in terms of
time and money. Capitol Hill has enough interesting places to eat that
we can meet any student's desire! A few years ago I had lunch with a
student in a cafe somewhere between her work and my office. As we
talked about her reading and the questions that had arisen in the first
weeks of the program, she exclaimed: "This isn't like school. My room-
mates and I have been up until two every night talking about class! This
is not just academic! This is about my life . . . my future . . . the future of
the world!"

With great enthusiasm she captured what we aim for in explicitly
exploring the question, How do I make sense of all this, personally and
publicly? She understood precisely how high the stakes are raised, if we
take a question like that seriously. And yet isn't that what is so lamen-
table about most education today? As Ernest Boyer has asked, so percep-
tively seeing into the frailty of university education in the late twentieth
century, "Education for what purpose? Competence toward what end?"[7]

The questions of purpose and end are woven into the fabric of our
effort, as we understand that the deepest lessons are not learned in text-
books, but instead are discovered as learning meets life. We work at that
on three levels:

1) the questions that shape our semester are the questions of life
   in the world;

2) studying current policy debates allows students to see that "ideas
   have legs;" and

3) the internship experience is a setting in which students can try to
   connect belief to behavior.

In each we have defined the relation of teacher to student in ways that allow the student to learn alongside the teacher; it is a commitment that comes from our deepest principles about the nature of knowing and the meaning of education.

We talk about the relationship between honest questions and honest answers. Written into the curriculum are questions that are basic to all humans, not just "Christian" questions. What do I believe? Is it true? What difference does it make, personally and publicly? In the first weeks of the program, these questions are taken very seriously, and they shape our study: the lectures, the books, the articles, the guest lecturers— all serve to open eyes to the meaning of those questions. At the end of the semester, we conclude our study by raising the questions again, asking "How would we answer them differently after four months together?" Intentionally, it is "our study," as these are questions for teacher and student alike, so we ask and answer them together.

Since the substance of the semester is spent on understanding the policy debates of the moment in the city, every semester is different. In one month-long unit we will study the "family values" rhetoric in the election, in another we will study the long-term prospects for peace in Somalia, and in yet another we will try to understand the "bite-the-bullet" nature of a meaningful deficit reduction plan. Intentionally, the language here is "we" as the issues are new to everyone, faculty and student alike. As teachers, we think that the best learning takes place when *everyone* is learning. For that reason we refer to ourselves as "senior members" and the students as "junior members" of our educational community.

Students spend twenty to twenty-five hours a week out in the world, interning in places that hold some vocational interest for them. Washington is a wonderful classroom for just that reason, with an incredible variety of possibilities. But most critical to an excellent placement is finding a supervisor who will give time and energy to the student. One of the words we use most often is "substantial," as it speaks to the high expectation we have of the kind of work our students usually get the opportunity to do. That opportunity, though, is directly related to a wonderful network of "adjunct professors" we have all over the city who supervise our students in their internships. The best among them open their lives to the students, allowing them to understand the commitments and passions that have shaped their vocational visions.

It is not perfect. Every semester we strain over expectations and communication, characteristically finding that our best efforts are not

good enough. People get mad and sad, both senior and junior members.
And yet typically we hear from students that their time with us was "the
most stimulating part of their undergraduate education." We are convinced that the deepest reason for that is that we have structured an educational community that requires that faculty and students learn together.
When that happens, education is more than academic and is worth staying up until the wee hours of the night, talking about class—of all things.

Notes on a Long-Loved Teacher:
Incarnational Education at its Finest

Recently my wife and I were invited to dinner in a beautiful eighteenth-
century home overlooking the Potomac River. But better than the place,
was the company. Many were friends, the people whose lives are twined
together with ours in worship, in our children's school, and in our vocations. Though we work in different places, we are all here in Washington
because we think that God has called us here.

We had gathered, not to "celebrate ourselves"—as foolish as that is
in any city, Washington seems full of it—but to honor a friend. Donald
Drew is not a household name, but he was dear to all in attendance. For
many years a master in an English boy's school, he became part of the
L'Abri community in Switzerland in the late sixties. Only one among us
had been formally his student; the rest of us had been drawn to him either
at L'Abri or through his writings because of the integrity of his life.[8]

After dinner, each of us around the thirty-foot table told tales of
Donald. What impressed me as I watched and listened was that Donald
had offered himself to each of us, making us feel unique and deserving of
his special attention. Though our stories were different, we all looked at
him with great warmth. One gave thanks for nursing him through the flu
(while still pony-tailed and passionate and not yet a Christian), one gave
thanks for a wife (at a critical point, Donald encouraged them to pursue
each another), one for his present job (Donald's recommendation had
been decisive), one for helping him to watch films critically (Donald's
model of mature Christian reflection on contemporary culture had
"freed" him at an important point), and yet another for encouraging him
to finish his Ph.D (Donald kept writing him notes telling him his work
was important and to "keep at it").

In a hundred different ways Donald had drawn us into his life and, in doing so, had fanned into flame visions and vocations worth pursuing with our hearts and minds. As he allowed us to know him, we came to know something of ourselves and our place in the world.

At the end of the evening, Donald's last words had to do with "clay feet" and "soli deo gloria." We understood, and we loved him all the more.

Notes

1. Stott has written widely over the last thirty years; his recent books include: *The Message of the Sermon on the Mount* (Downer's Grove: InterVarsity, 1985), *The Cross of Christ* (Downer's Grove: InterVarsity, 1986), *Decisive Issues Facing Christians Today* (Old Tappan: Revell, 1990), *The Spirit, the Church and the World: The Message of Acts* (Downer's Grove: InterVarsity, 1990), *The Contemporary Christian* (Downer's Grove: InterVarsity, 1992).

2. Thomas Hughes, *Tom Brown's School Days* (New York: Signet, 1986), 126.

3. All quotations from the Bible are from the *NIV* (Grand Rapids: Zondervan, 1978).

4. See G. J. Botterweck and H. Ringren (eds.), *Theological Dictionary of the Old Testament,* Vol. 5 (Grand Rapids: Eerdmans, 1986), 448-481.

5. For information about the American Studies Program, including course syllabi, write: American Studies Program, 327 8th Street NE, Washington, DC 20002.

6. S. Hauerwas, "Self-Deception and Autobiography: Reflections on Speer's *Inside the Third Reich, Truthfulness and Tragedy"* (Notre Dame: University of Notre Dame, 1977), 82-98.

7. E. Boyer, *College: The Undergraduate Experience in America* (New York: Harper & Row, 1987), 283.

8. His best known writing is *Images of Man: A Critique of the Contemporary Cinema* (Downer's Grove: InterVarsity, 1974).

Questions for Discussion

1. What is at the heart of the themes, revelation and response? What did you learn about this from the story about Tom Brown and Dr. Arnold?

2. Why does the teaching of Jesus only make sense if we appreciate Jesus', and the general Hebrew, understanding of knowledge?

3. How does Jesus' identification of discipleship as apprenticeship affect our understanding of teaching? Connect this to the earlier themes of revelation and response.

4. Evaluate the American Studies Program's efforts to link life with learning in light of the themes of revelation and response. If a teacher, how does your vision for your vocation connect to these themes?

IX.
The Farmer as Re-Settler: Cultivating and Connecting in the Real World

Richard Begbie

On a parched summer afternoon in 1982, at the height of the drought gripping most of rural Australia, a familiar scene unfolded at one farm gate. A large mob of sheep, with horses, drovers, and dogs surged through the gateway onto the ungrazed pastures of the roadside, the legendary *long paddock* of the Australian countryside.

This was a family farm, and the drovers were mother, father, and children, with a couple of friends along for the experience. After eighteen months without rain, this was their only alternative to denuding soil, slaughtering stock, or borrowing money for drought-priced fodder. For three months they wandered after grass and water, camping at night, and living the timeless lives of shepherds.

A typical enough story of country Australia, but one with a twist to it all the same. That farm gate is less than thirty miles from Parliament House in central Canberra. The mother and father were both children of the twentieth century city, having moved to the country only a decade before.

In that thirty-mile arc around the nation's capital lie thousands of small farms occupied by new settlers. This is no isolated phenomenon. Most Australian cities and large towns have seen a similar growth over the past couple of decades. Urban middle-class people throughout the Western world have been migrating in droves to some kind of rural or semi-rural alternative.

What lies behind this quiet pilgrimage? Is it middle-class indulgence or an eager search for the image in which we were made? What, if anything, has it done for the pilgrims?

Answers can be found at many levels, and because they deal in the diverse and contrary stuff of human nature, explanations are both complex

and contradictory. The sociologist, demographer, and theologian look
for common threads to suggest trends, tribal values, and spiritual meaning. But for the rural pilgrims themselves, these generalities are usually
less-than-satisfying.

For those who have set out to discover a new (or is it very old?)
relationship with creation, the answers that count arise from personal
experience. That in turn depends on the attitudes and beliefs that inform
the new life. For one young Christian in 1972, the change began a radical reevaluation. Much of what follows stems from the experience and
mind-set I took to the country.

I was an unlikely settler. Childhood friends and family often set out
from our Sydney suburb in the 1950s for farm holidays. I had never
stayed on a farm overnight before the summer of 1972, when we packed
our few belongings and trundled from inner Sydney into a new universe.
On our first night I had little sleep: the depth and immensity of the
silence was profoundly disturbing. (My wife, Carla, welcomed the quiet
like a homecoming and slept deep and sound.)

In fact as a new settler I was a fraud. I had no real interest in
country life. Our move was in response to a *call*, in the orthodox Protestant jargon of the day. The call was invariably to some overtly Christian
ministry. This, although no one ever said so out loud, put the person
who was called into a different category from ordinary Christians, who
merely had jobs. Our call was to a ministry amongst young people, and
for various reasons we had decided that the country would provide a
good setting.

In fact, with the help of others, we did set up a community for young
people. The experiences we had over seven years were formative for us
all, though they won't come much into this story. Our present interest
lies more in the effect of the move on a well-educated, opinionated
product of the sixties such as I was, a remote figure now in more ways
than one.

As our project unfolded, puzzling bells began to sound, quiet at first
and then with such persistent clamor that even the self-assured young
man was forced to pay attention. Instead of being merely a good backdrop for full-time ministry, farming began to insinuate itself as a way of
life. The first hints of a revolution to stir my all-knowing complacency
came with an exhilarating discovery.

I found that the simple activities of farming and stockwork, regulated by night and day, spring and high summer, touched my soul in a way I never expected. As Carla and our small child had done at once, I slowly began to sense my own homecoming in ways that I, so fluent with words and explanations, found hard to articulate, let alone understand.

I first became aware of it one evening in the fall, at that hour before dusk when the cool night air is beginning to settle in layers on the creek flats. The farming novice who knew so much had just finished his first day's plowing, and on a whim switched off the old Fordson and looked back over the newly turned ground. The steady diesel growl had left a deep silence in its wake, which somehow opened another dimension. The black soil was moist, still warm, a living organism with the mystery of new life pressed in every furrow. Satisfaction in work worth doing expanded into a sense of oneness with the rich granite earth, of a seemly and seamless fit.

It was not something I had sought or expected. In time I recognized a similar sense in a hundred experiences: In (for example) the intuitive co-operation of man and working dog or the aching limbs and home-brewed beer and easy talk around the stack after a day's haycarting. It came with the physical delight of a meal homegrown and nurtured from seed to table, and it pierced the soul when my small child stabbed a wondering finger at the dawn sky: "Hey look Dad! The morning star!"

Later on and more slowly it emerged in the minor key, when lambs were stillborn and a bullock slaughtered for rations. The smug confidence born of youth and a closed-system faith gave way to a new impulse; the urge to actually understand what was happening in our ancient new life, and how God was acting through it. This was a slower process still. It goes on as I write and will do so for a lifetime.

Paradoxically, it leads away from the idiosyncrasies that make our story different, toward discoveries familiar to most new settlers. Though life spins them into a single web, I shall try to tease out four kinds of relationships, devalued and often lost in an urban, techno-industrial society, but made possible in new ways on the farm. They are our relations to each other, to the land, to ourselves, and to God.

Each Other

The community we discovered in 1972 was only lightly dusted with the glitter of the twentieth century. On its small family farms the motor car had not been common twenty years before, and a trip to the local town was an event that meant careful planning and dressing up. The electricity supply was only ten years old, and we still wound a handle on the telephone to rouse Lorna, our exchange operator.

Europeans had ruled the valley for more than a century when we, a second alien wave, rolled into the world they'd fashioned. Their community and culture were already disintegrating, though the dying echoes of how it had been for generations still sounded clear. We listened with the intensity of tourists, making the same glib, patronizing observations. The Europeans had viewed the Aborigines as backward savages, and my attitude toward the older settlers was not so different. But I was unaware (like most invaders) of my arrogance.

With youthful condescension and urban wisdom we smiled at what we saw, yet we understood little of the world of our new neighbors. In time we came to look beyond simple speech and quaint anachronisms to older, deeper patterns: a rich network of family and social relations, a scale of values that paid some heed to money and little to time as we measured it, and attitudes to the land that would take the urban cowboy a lifetime to unravel.

An early lesson in these values came with our first venture into livestock. The merino sheep with its fine, soft wool is well adapted to the grazing lands of our region. However, the merino needs careful management, including a *crutching* in late fall, when stained and dirty wool is shorn away from the sheep's crutch. We had no mechanically driven hand-piece, only a pair of hand shears known affectionately in the sheep country as *blades*. At first I enjoyed myself in the old woolshed, enveloped in the rich lanoline smell of the greasy wool. But after an hour my back was on fire and the spring in the blades had reduced my forearm to a throbbing pulp. After four hours I was near despair, with forty sheep done and sixty more to go.

It was about then that the old Land Rover pulled up at the shed, and our neighbor Frank ambled in. "Doin' a bit, eh Richard? Seen you was crutchin' earlier on, and thought I'd see how yer goin'." He surveyed my meager efforts. "They look good, too."

Painfully straightening my back, I grinned. Nothing like a compliment from an old hand. Little did I realize he'd almost certainly measured my progress from afar, and knew I had no hope of finishing before dark.

"Got the old blades in the Rover," he went on. "Would it be interferin' if I gave you a hand?" My grin broadened. Would it what! We finished them in an hour, and how that hour flew. Frank knew I was done in, and stopped me often, ostensibly to sharpen the blades. "Just touch 'em up a bit fer yer," he'd say. I'd start in again, trying to work faster to keep up my end and my image. "Steady on Richard," he'd drawl. "Yer'll get me flustered. Never done a day's work in me life, and don't intend to start now."

As the last sheep disappeared into the yard my gratitude knew no bounds. Frank grinned from under a battered felt hat. "I enjoyed it," he said. "Anyhow, you'll do the same fer me some day."

By such easy steps were we introduced to a framework of relationship that owed more to the New Testament than the ethos of individual rights and free enterprise. At the busy times of shearing and haymaking, in the emergencies of accident, fire, or flood, Frank's casual enactment of the second great commandment found endless variants and suggested new ways of relating.

Another kind of relationship emerged early on too. Max and Betty would become the closest of friends, but before that Max was my mentor. His entire life had unfolded in the valley. Interrupted only briefly by a simple homestead education, it consisted of farming the valley floor, running sheep in the forbidding ranges around, and preserving a family heritage rooted in that granite soil.

We were an unlikely pair, the voluble, well-educated, urban hick and his shy, stammering, country guide. The simple matters of daily living for which a lifetime of education had failed to prepare me were second nature to the unassuming Max, who worked his way patiently through the alien's profound ignorance. Again it was years before I understood the significance of his role as counselor, guide, and friend.

Then there were family relationships. Our children began to grow up removed from a society that devours without thought of true cost and consumes the trinkets of the age without understanding. And we grew with them. The children breached easily the watertight compartments of my urban mind: work was not some mysterious task undertaken by parents, any more than play was a discrete activity for them. We all took part in both, according to strength and ability.

Tennis was something we all enjoyed, for example, but there would never be money for a tennis court, so we built one together. Sweat was produced in the building and then in the playing, but which was work and which play? Photographs of the hilarity and clowning that were a feature of the project make it hard to say.

The sense of being in it together also brought us naturally to the questions of role and gender that have convulsed society at large. Household chores, like most farm jobs, were shared from when the children were young. Off-farm income, important when wool prices are low, has mostly come from Carla's teaching work, and this has pushed the most inept of us into the full range of household duties.

Carla's training as scientist and instinct as nurturer make her especially imaginative and thoughtful in farm management decisions. So the divisions in family authority and responsibility with which we grew up have been radically reshaped by our move to the real world.

Sadly, our arrival in the country coincided with the turn of the tide. Even as we began to glimpse and absorb these patterns they were disintegrating. The values shaping the urban world had already encroached far onto the rural fabric. Agribusiness was the buzz word of the day, and our neighbors were being told to get big or get out. Either alternative would shatter community ties and individual hearts, as so many were to discover.[1]

The accumulated knowledge and shared history thus lost cannot be replaced by a degree or a welfare program. We, like others who cherish it, have tried to retain the continuity, the stability, the eager hospitality of that world. It finds reflection these days in our annual woolshed dance, where a mixed crowd of family, friends, and neighbors gather for home-grown dancing, entertainment, and supper. To watch a new generation, bewildered at first without "professional" musicians and entertainers, gradually discover what ordinary people can do together, is to find real hope.

The Land

In those early days I took pleasure in the edge given to the Bible's pastoral imagery by life on the farm. Isaiah's "sheep silent before her shearers," Hosea's "stubborn heifer," the hundreds of uses of the "sowing" and "reaping" image all came to life. Much later I realized that these were not just handy pictures for the Old Testament prophets, for Jesus and Paul. These images were the deepest expression of an agrarian people's struggle to know the mind and nature of God. Their physical world would shape everything that came after.

My brief moments of illumination had little to do with the knowledge I had brought from the education process. That dealt in neat answers, predictable quantities, and repeatable results. *Objective* and *scientific* were its favorite words, and I was eager to *know* farming in this sense. My mentor, Max, was confronted with a young man who wanted to add farming to his knowledge portfolio.

My questions (and there were plenty) were all of the "how much?", "how many?", and "how soon?" variety. How much milk should we get from this cow? How many bales of alfalfa will this field produce? How long will it take us to break in this mare? How many lambs will we get from our hundred ewes? Max would look puzzled, and say little.

One evening as we rode home, my chatter and endless questions filling the dusk silence, he stopped abruptly and turned with his hand raised like a policeman to stem the flow. "It all depends," he said, and rode on. I barely paused: My neat economy of knowledge had room for a few variables. "Depends on what?"

So in the half-light and to an all-knowing citizen of the globe, Max hesitantly began to unfold the contingent and unpredictable ways of God's world, which he had learned without ever leaving that hidden valley. And I too paused at last, catching a glimpse of another way of knowing. The illusions of a generation, an entire civilization, were exploded by Max's three words.

It depends on rain and warmth, on frost and wind, on temperament, your neighbors, health, climate change. It doesn't depend on your Dad's income, or the stock market, or the weather forecaster, or the government. Dollars and schedules and income and GNP are merely props, constructs concealing the ultimate and true sources of our dependence.

With this epiphany came understanding of the great gulf that

Wendell Berry was later to write about, between exploiter and nurturer. The one, with projections made according to calculator and ambitious profit margins, asks all the questions that Max endured. The nurturer or steward is more interested in the carrying capacity of the land than its maximum yield, in its health and that of the bodies and souls it sustains than greater profit margins.

Max's revelation pointed to a value system that distinguishes the important and basic from the urgent and trivial. An Australian wheat farmer went last year to buy basketball shoes for his teenage son. He had to sell two tons of wheat to make the purchase: enough wheat for say 2,000 loaves of bread, in exchange for sport shoes that will last his growing son a season. Modern society has lost even a meager cerebral understanding of "It all depends."

Closer to home, Carla has pointed out that of our 400 acres, about five around the homestead are devoted to our own supplies, namely, fruit, vegetables, honey, meat, eggs, milk, butter, and the rest. Careful stewardship should enable us to grow enough timber for fuel and some building as well. The remainder (395 acres), mostly light grazing country, supports the extras of a relatively modest Western lifestyle, and if we treat it unkindly it won't even do that. A true knowledge of our dependence brings a responsibility the affluent West has either expunged from memory or has chosen to ignore.

But the knowledge into which I was initiated that evening doesn't just bring responsibility. It brings the sweet scent of new-mown hay, the steady rhythm of the morning milking, and the quiet arguments of chickens roosting at dusk. It brings the devastation of a lost crop or dead calf, the awesome power of fire and flood. There is pleasure in producing and satisfaction in the product. And as true knowledge increases, so does an awed wonder at the endless variety, the infinite permutations of the factors on which we all depend.

To Ourselves

Early in 1940, C. S. Lewis wrote to his brother, serving with the army in France. Warren Lewis had been a regular member of the Inklings, the informal group that met around his brother to talk, read aloud, and fraternize. He would have enjoyed news of that week's gathering, "an

evening almost equally compounded of merriment, piety and literature."
In a laconic aside Lewis went on:

> The Inklings is now really very well provided, with Adam Fox as
> chaplain, you as army, Barfield as lawyer, Harvard as doctor—
> almost all the estates—except of course anyone who could actually
> produce a single necessity of life—a loaf, a boot, or a hut . . . .[2]

In a more serious vein, Lewis often lamented his ineptitude in practical matters, and most new settlers, however adept with their hands, will
all know something of that frustration. Because suddenly they discover
the need for skills and ingenuity that (like Lewis) they suspect they don't
have.

The age of the specialist, we tend to feel, has freed us from all that.
The specialist can make or mend anything. When something goes wrong
with the car, plumbing, or digestive system, our automatic response has
become not "How do I fix it?" or even "What's wrong?" but "Who do I
call?"

Some of the most vivid memories of our early days on the farm
center on the waves of helplessness engulfing us as we gazed at the burst
water pipe, the inconsolable child, the laboring cow down and unable to
deliver, the dead tractor. Is the phone working? (Often it wasn't.), and
who would come out anyway? We felt the helplessness of a race that has
handed over to the specialist. Not just for micro-surgery or genetic en-
gineering, but for food, clothing, and shelter.

Like most new settlers, we learned from necessity. As we did, we
began to take absurd pleasure in sheltering under a roof we'd pitched,
eating our own produce, turning on the tap of a water supply we'd in-
stalled. Maybe it seemed absurd because we had not yet learned respect
for the knowledge and experience that goes into sound building and wise
stewardship of the earth. With our peers we had reduced that wisdom to
dollars and cents.

As time went on, we gained confidence and discovered new abilities
within ourselves. Carla, for example, had an uncanny way with broken-
down machinery. The reclaiming of skills basic to survival brought a
new sense, not only of control, but also of what can best be described as
personhood. Backyard carpenters, home spinners and weavers, and
vegetable gardeners will often surprise themselves in the same way.

What our era dismisses as merely a hobby is often a practical step towards restoring wholeness.

For the Christian the reason for this serendipitous discovery is not hard to find. Each of us retains something of the image in which we were made, the image of a creator. The echo of the creative spirit atrophies if it is not heeded, and the age of the specialist has done much to stifle it. Anything that reverses the process is a step towards our healing and re-fashioning in God's image.

To God

For years now we have been trying to re-establish trees on our over-cleared grazing lands. Soil erosion, the need for shade and shelter, and especially the need to restore the diverse and robust ecosystems that once gave our tired soil its health, all make this project vital. However it is a terrific struggle. What a few axe-strokes achieved a century ago is bafflingly difficult to reverse. Every year a new insect, disease, or set of seasonal conditions brings some of our work undone. The further we delve into it, the more we realize we don't know.

The depth of our ignorance is clear to anyone who attempts a serious understanding of the natural world. For the Christian, ignorance challenges any facile or simplistic teaching of God as creator. God does not, as the old saying claims, temper the wind to the shorn lamb. There appears to be as much caprice as goodwill, chaos as order, in God's world.

On the other hand, there are intimations of something other, more glorious and powerful than we can bear. One scorching summer day I set out early to muster sheep in the ranges nearby. The dogs were keen, my stocky little mare fresh, and I was young and invincible. By high noon all that had changed. It was one hundred degrees plus, we hadn't come across a sheep in hours of battling the thick scrub, and the water bottle in my saddlebag was empty.

With the weary farmer in a state of terminal exasperation, we suddenly broke into a small clearing high up on the range, empty apart from a single tree, the gnarled skeleton of an ancient eucalyptus. At eye level on a low limb, not twenty yards from us, perched a superb adult wedge-tailed eagle. Did I pull the mare up or was she also transfixed by the vision? I only know that we stopped, with the dogs in our shade, gazing at the soaring monarch brought close and still.

The eagle returned our gaze and it was my heart that soared, as for a moment out of time it seemed possible for us to reach out and touch. How long did we sit, thus linked? Thirty seconds? Five minutes? I have no idea. Maybe eternal things are only possible outside our cramping measures of time. Then the eagle leaned forward, unfolded those mighty wings in slow motion, and flew with a rush of air from sight.

The passage from Isaiah came to mind, and our strength was indeed renewed: that afternoon we ran, and were not weary (Isaiah 40.31). But there was another passage too, on the edge of thought. Ah yes, "the creation waits with eager longing for the revealing of the sons of God." The "groaning in travail" of creation is a common enough experience, but the naturalist and hiker will gladly testify to these occasional moments of transcendence when that "eager longing" seems close to being satisfied (Rom. 8.19-23).

If I had to single out the central hallmark of the new settler's experience, threading together all of these discoveries, it would be the profound sense of connectedness I experienced on that mountain. The family and community that works and plays together, firsthand contact with the real sources of human dependence, and growth towards personal wholeness in making and mending, all join in a seamless whole to connect the believer with family, friends, and God.

A footnote and I am done.

You don't have to move to the country to work these things out. It took that upheaval to pierce my confident armor, but more alert people discover the important things in ordinary urban surroundings. My dawning recognition owed much to family memory of a suburban yard where my parents ran chickens and brewed compost alongside a vegetable patch, vines, and fruit trees. An old shed where boots were mended and furniture made should not be forgotten.

On the other hand, going rural guarantees nothing. A study I undertook in 1986 revealed a whole class of new settlers whose primary interest is a more imposing yard and sweeping view.[3] Soil structure only becomes important when they go to excavate for their pool, and the shiny four wheel drive wagon is for town display more than farm use. These settlers have successfully combined the worst of both worlds.

The vital message is that these discoveries be made: it does not matter much where.

Notes

1. Wendell Berry, *The Unsettling of America: Culture and Agriculture* (New York: Avon, 1978), 39-48.

2. W. H. Lewis (ed.), *Letters of C. S. Lewis* (London: Geoffrey Bles, 1966), 176.

3. Richard Begbie, *The Move to the Land* (Unpublished thesis 1986, held at the Australian National University), 11-12.

Questions for Discussion

1. How would the farmer go about differentiating between the spiritual and secular part of his or her life?

2. What have we lost with the disintegration of older rural communities? Are those values and experiences recoverable in other contexts?

3. As we see from passages like Gen.3:5; Is.47:8, and Jer. 16:21, the Old Testament notion of knowledge is very different from ours. Has our perspective changed as a result of this shift in meaning?

4. Do you think there are any connections between first-hand responsi bility for the things on which we depend and our relationship with God? If so, what are they, and how can we go about making them?

X.
A Craftworker as Marketplace Apostle: Forming a Co-operative on Early Church Principles

Julia Banks

The Birth of a Business Venture

It was monsoon month in the Banks' household. It seemed that every time my husband and I talked, I ended up in tears.

I was thirty-four years old, the mother of two boys in elementary school and the wife of a university lecturer. Eighteen months earlier we'd moved from one city to another because of my husband's work. I had chosen not to continue my work toward a Bachelor of Education degree because of the impact that would have on the quality of our family life. I chose to occupy myself outside the home with visiting elderly relatives, getting to know the neighbors, and becoming involved in our boys' school, preparing lunches, hearing slow learners read, and attending the Parents and Citizens Association.

The first year-and-a-half passed quickly; I thought I was happy until the new year dawned, and I was faced with the prospect of another twelve months of the same activities. That's when the monsoons set in! I hasten to add that my husband was a wonderful friend, helping me to explore all the possible options. Inevitably these discussions led to the same conclusion: I needed more training or education, the very thing I did not want to do because I wanted to spend time with my family.

"Isn't there anything among all the things you do now that you could expand into something more?" asked my husband one afternoon. "Of all the things you have been doing in the last few months what has given you the most satisfaction?"

I didn't have to think twice, although my response was a long way from the academic and professional pursuits I'd been considering. "I really enjoyed making those soft toys and puppets for our nephews and nieces for Christmas."

"Well then," my husband responded, hopeful that a solution was in view, "as well as making them for relatives, why don't you find an outlet through which you can sell them?"

It sounded so simple, but I knew that I didn't have the self-esteem to risk the rejection I would feel if no one wished to buy them.

What follows is my story of the link between the marketplace and God's work. My past experience in church-related activities had a tremendous effect on how I found my place in the world of work, and my entrepreneurial adventure was shaped largely because of my conviction about God's role in our activities.

A couple of weeks after we had discussed the possibility of my making a career in handcrafts, my husband asked me if I'd noticed that one of the little stores opposite the school was for rent. "Why don't you start a craft shop?" he asked.

I snorted at the impracticality of the idea. "What would I use for capital?" Having recently taken out a large mortgage, we were barely making ends meet as it was, and we certainly didn't have any savings.

But the idea was planted and in the middle of the night I awoke. "What if I started a craft shop and took others' crafts on consignment?" That would take care of the need for a large capital outlay. "What if I involved others in the running of the shop?" That would prevent it from becoming too time consuming. None of us would have to be at the shop every day, and we could cover for each other when children were sick and when we wanted to take holidays.

My mind raced, seeing difficulties and finding solutions. By breakfast I was ready to try out the idea on my husband. With his encouragement I spent the day calling an accountant, the real estate agent, and city hall. Each person I spoke to mentioned something that allowed me to ask a further question; gradually my picture of what was involved in getting a shop started was expanded.

Within a couple of days I had drawn up a "prospectus" and costed the operation. Was I crazy? My only retail experience, apart from that of a consumer, was six weeks behind a counter in Woolworth's when I was fifteen! I had some experience working in a bank, so I wasn't totally ignorant or frightened of money and accounting, as I soon discovered many of the craft people were.

The next question was where was I going to find the people to join me in the venture. The only other person I knew who had craft interests was a woman who lived several doors down the street. I felt very nervous about approaching her, particularly since I recently had said no when she suggested that I start a Bible study group for neighbors. That had not been an easy decision to make. Part of me felt obliged to say yes, but a bigger part of me screamed out no. Though it sounded selfish I felt very strongly that whatever I did at this point in my life had to be for me. So having said no to her request to join her in ministry how could I now ask her to join me in my self-interest?

The moment came, however, when I felt God say to me, "This is it!" Though I didn't realize it at the time, it was a *kairos* moment. My neighbor listened patiently and asked some good questions. If she had scoffed at the idea, that would have ended everything. But she didn't.

The Starting of a Craft Shop

The following week my neighbor and I invited everyone we knew with an interest in crafts to a meeting at my house. There were seven at the first gathering, twelve at the next, and so our numbers gradually grew. We felt we needed about seventy people to properly staff the venture. The group was made up mainly of housewives, college students and retirees, few of whom had any business experience.

One of those who attended the first meeting had a friend involved in a craft co-operative in another suburb and offered to find out what she could about how that functioned. The people in that co-operative were very responsive, and we owe a large debt to them for their generous support and encouragement. They allowed us to use their constitution as a guide for our own. We were also able to learn from their struggles as well as their successes.

Three months later our shop opened, not opposite the school but in the regional shopping center. Being upstairs, on a side street, and on the edges of a main development, it was not a prime location. Our initial membership was about fifty; shortly after opening, our numbers soon swelled. That meant that we could have two people in the shop each day, with each craft person working one day per month. This kept operating costs down and meant that a bigger percentage of the sales price could go to the craft producer.

We decided to give any profits left over when costs had been deducted from the income to local charities. We also agreed to have a "show" once a year, exhibiting our best work, with the proceeds donated to charity, for example, the children's ward at the local hospital.

The co-operative's membership was divided into smaller groups according to crafts produced. The various groups represented were: potters, leather workers, spinners and weavers, embroiderers and soft toy makers, silversmiths and jewellers, and a miscellaneous group.

Each of the craft groups was responsible for the quality and pricing of the goods they made. For example, if someone was applying to join the co-operative as a leather worker, the leather workers group decided whether there was a need for more wares in their area, whether the goods were sufficiently different from those made by other members, and whether the quality was of the required standard. Each craft group also selected a member to represent it's interests at the meeting of the executive committee of the co-operative.

The executive committee was selected by vote of the membership and consisted of a president, secretary, treasurer, membership secretary, public relations officer, and the craft representatives. I was asked to be the president and remained in that position for the first three years. The executive committee met monthly, although there was a lot of business conducted by phone in the intervening weeks.

The Principles of Our Operation

The idea of managing a large group of people through small group work was not new to me. I had been introduced to it as a Girl Scout. The patrol system was used to help new recruits feel connected, to provide teams where members learned to depend on each others' skills to serve a common goal, and to allow older members to take responsibility for teaching younger ones what they needed to know to pass their various tests.

My husband and I had used a similar model in our work as church youth group leaders, dividing the large group into smaller ones, providing them with tasks to do, and encouraging the older, more experienced, members to take an active interest in younger, newer ones. In that way we hoped to train future leaders. The older members, or elders, met with us to make decisions about the life of the fellowship as a whole.

But it was through my involvement over a ten year period with a cluster of small house churches that I learned the most about living in community, and from which I drew valuable guidance in establishing and managing the co-operative. These house churches consisted of groups of twelve to sixteen people—married couples, singles, and children. Once a week we would meet for three to four hours in a member's home for informal worship and the opportunity to learn to be a genuine Christian family. Every few weeks members of the various house churches gathered for a combined celebration, generally lasting half a day or longer.

The house church model was based on a rather rudimentary understanding of what the New Testament said about the character and practices of the early church. As we sought to follow those guidelines, we found ourselves returning again and again to the Bible for new insight. The teachings of Paul came alive in a way we had never dreamed possible as we learned to appreciate the wisdom, relevance, and practicality of his advice to the infant Church.

Over the years I had seen so many worthwhile endeavours (both inside and outside of the Church) come to nothing because of unnecessary tensions brought on by competition, lack of trust, and self-interest. How could I translate what I had learned in the Church into principles and practices that would be acceptable to a body of people from all walks of life and with a mixture of belief systems? Sensing that it would be unacceptable to quote the Bible, I decided to employ the language of grass-roots democracy and community.

I did not have to work hard to introduce these concepts. On the whole the members of the co-operative were people of goodwill. Most suggestions I made gained ready acceptance and some were improved. Once the basic ethos was set, members came forward with ideas to strengthen our direction. From the outset the whole adventure was very much a group process.

Let me identify some of the basic principles I was able to transfer into our co-operative business venture from my experience with the house churches.

It is important to eat and drink together. In the New Testament we are introduced to the Lord's Supper as a full meal. In Acts 2:42, in the period immediately following Pentecost, we see a picture of the early believers gathering together to break bread, shorthand for saying that they shared a meal. It was belonging to a house church that helped me see the centrality of the meal. We celebrated the Lord's Supper in the context of a full meal to which every one brought a contribution. As we ate the meal together we shared our lives. I don't fully understand why that sharing was so successful. Perhaps it was the leisurely pace of eating which allowed time for people to interact. Perhaps the food itself provided something to talk about to ease the awkward moments, or perhaps there was something about taking food from common bowls that united us. Each meal was a sort of parable that when we came together we each had something to contribute to the others' well-being.

In the co-operative it wasn't possible to have a meal each time we met, but we did begin each meeting of the executive committee and of the whole body with socializing and refreshments. The small groups were encouraged to include a meal with their monthly meetings. This helped to establish a web of strong relationships which helped to defuse tensions when areas of contention arose. Group leaders also were encouraged to keep a caring eye on their members and to inform us all if anyone was sick or needed help of any kind.

Each member of the co-operative has a contribution to make. Through those passages of the Bible which speak of the church as the body of Christ (Rom. 12.4ff.; 1 Cor. 12:12ff.; Eph. 4:11), I had learned that everyone had a contribution to make to our life together. While some may have more to contribute than others, none is more important than the others. I had also learned that our contributions varied in character and that this was not only good but important. The more varied the contributions, the richer our life together, and the more we were built up into the fullness of Christ. Even our weaknesses were gifts, enabling the church to grow in love, patience, faithfulness, and wisdom, stretching our imaginations and helping us not to take ourselves too seriously.

People feel free to contribute only when there is an atmosphere of love and trust. The whole person must be valued, not simply his or her gift. This made the need for "wasting" time over meals all the more important, particularly in the craft groups where people were encouraged to develop a spirit of genuine co-operation. Among other things, this meant people sharing their private craft techniques so that they could learn from each other and improve the quality of their crafts.

Decisions are made by the group. There were many occasions in house church when members suffered severe frustration at the time required to give everbody a say in the making of decisions. We were, however, committed to the principle. And not simply because we believed that it was consistent with the teaching of Paul (see Acts 16.10; 1 Cor.5.4), nor because it gave equal value to all the members. Frankly, we did it because it worked. When everyone owns a decision it can be implemented much more quickly and without a lot of resistance and complaint. The decision may take more time to make but what follows takes much less time.

It was hard to get consensus in a group the size of the co-operative, but I was committed to getting each member to participate fully in the decision making. All major decisions were made at meetings of the entire membership, requiring agreement by a two-thirds majority. At the executive committee meetings we would look ahead to what decisions needed to be made and examine options and consequences. Then it was the responsibilty of the craft group leaders to discuss these with their group members so that people were able to vote intelligently. The craft leaders were also asked to report any complaints that members had so that these could be addressed before they became major issues.

Look for leadership within the group. This was perhaps the hardest principle, for no matter how hard you try, once you've used the word "leadership" those influenced by our Western culture immediately think of someone out front who is over the rest. This is not, however, the Biblical understanding of leadership. Christ is the only Lord of the Church. He is the head of the body and we are members of it; our task is to serve the head and each other. Nevertheless, as in the early churches (1 Cor. 16.19ff.; 1 Th. 5.12ff.), it is true that within each house church there emerged what we called a pastoral center. This was made up of a small group of people who cared not just for the individuals in the group, but for the group as a whole. These people often fulfilled their roles in an inconspicuous manner. They weren't necessarily the traditional leadership types, rather, they were most often characterized by faith, hope, and love.

I tried to allow this concept of leadership to inform my role as president of the co-operative. I saw my presidential role as one of enabling, by encouraging a vision of what the co-operative could be. It wasn't simply my vision, though I did have a big influence on what emerged. It was more that I put forward an original vision that was flexible and encouraged others to have input so that it became a corporate vision. We all owned it.

My next task was to "pastor" those on the executive committee. I spent time with them as a group and as individuals, getting to know them, complementing them on their work, making suggestions, and encouraging them to take initiatives and risks. I learned from them and worked to develop mutual regard and co-operation. There were many occasions when I had to forfeit my own involvement in a particular aspect of the co-operative's operation so that others could have the opportunity to develop new talents. I was very conscious of the fact that the executive committee was a model for the craft groups. I made the executive committee my prime responsibility.

Ironically, individual gifts tend to emerge when the welfare of the whole group is the pre-eminent concern. Today most churches teach that individuals need to discover their gifts. As we wrestled with this teaching in house church, we found ourselves searching the Scriptures, studying the passages in Romans 12, 1 Corinthians 12-14, and Ephesians 4. We came to realize that God gives these gifts not for us individually so that we can each claim a possession, but rather "to each one the manifestation of the Spirit is given for the common good" (1 Cor. 12:7). And more, it's not just that the gift is given for the common good; when we look outside ourselves and actively seek the common good, gifts are given (1 Cor. 14:12). Time and time again in house church we witnessed the miracle of folk growing in love for one another, and through that love gifts emerged to meet the needs of others.

I don't know that it is possible to say that I or anyone else consciously set this principle in place in the craft co-operative. It was more a consequence of the process. That is, when folk actively sought the well-being of the whole group, they found themselves doing things they had never done before. My own experience is a good example.

The shop needed to advertise, but we really couldn't afford to do so. What were we to do? Our public relations officer came up with a bright idea. She went to the local newspaper to ask if our story was newsworthy. Fortunately it was, so a reporter came to the shop to interview a few of us and to take some photos. Little did we realize the impact this was to have!

Soon I found myself being interviewed and photographed by a number of regional newspapers. Soon after the largest metropolitan newspaper did a two-thirds of a page spread about the shop, featuring photos of me wearing products crafted by the members. Then came the

invitations to appear on television: one on a midday magazine-type
program for women, and the other a segment of a nationally produced
talk show. Next came an invitation to go on a morning radio call-in
program, which lead to a seminar for the YWCA on "How to Start a
Small Business." I couldn't believe this was happening to me, the woman who hesitantly started the co-operative with such low self-esteem
and who had been so lacking in confidence. My up-front, public speaking, and diplomacy skills were expanded rapidly.

Some Consequences of the Enterprise

There were several unexpected consequences of this whole venture.
    I came to recognize the value of my skills. For example, there were
the organizational skills that I had gained in that much-despised occupation as housewife. There were also those gained in house church,
namely, relational skills. But I wasn't the only one who began to recognize personal strengths and skills. All of the members of the co-operative did. As mentioned earlier, our co-operative was made up primarily
of housewives, college students, and retirees. We were a very ordinary
bunch of people, yet we found all sorts of abilities being drawn from us
as we worked for the common good.
    As time passed, it wasn't just each other's craft gifts we were en-
joying, it was the fruit of each others' lives. Within a month of the shop
opening, one of the members told me that she'd been able to throw away
her Valium. Others spoke eloquently of the friendships they had made or
the sense of purpose that they had gained. We were a happy band, a true
co-operative, and our life together was marked by very little discord. It
was a constant source of amazement to the members that we lived together in such harmony while other organizations were constantly in
conflict.
    The shop hadn't been open long before we became aware that some-
thing totally unexpected was happening. We had caught the public imagination. That was surely attested to by the way the media took up our
story! Over the weeks and months it became obvious that there were
some who came into the shop not so much to buy, as to look around, talk
with the members of the co-operative, and ask how things were going.
They were pleased to see this group of very ordinary people, with no

particular training in business, succeed in this adventure. These loyal friends gave us far more than they ever knew.

There were also people who needed someone to talk to and take an interest in them. They would simply wander in off the street, casually look around the shop, maybe purchase a gift, then fall into conversation with the person behind the counter and bring out all the day's troubles. It was a very humbling experience to be trusted with peoples' cares in that way. They weren't looking for counselling: all they needed was for someone to listen.

Finally, a further spin-off of the extraordinary publicity that the shop received was that we were contacted by others with similar interests. So we had the added pleasure of assisting people to set up the kind of enterprise that we had created. This happened not only in our own city but in other parts of the state. It didn't take us long to realize that we existed as much for others as we did for ourselves. This was a delightful bonus for us all. It was a special vindication for me, since I still had occasional doubts about refusing to lead the neighborhood Bible study.

Conclusion

Eventually we moved away from that city, but whenever I was in the vicinity I would visit to see how things were going. It was pleasing to hear that the foundations of the craft co-operative had proved durable over time. It is still in existence, though some years ago it had to forfeit the shop due to skyrocketing rents. Members' creations now are sold at local festivals and craft shows. The co-operative continues the practice of holding an annual craft exhibition and giving away all corporate profits to charitable institutions.

Questions for Discussion

1. Whether you are in the workforce or not, are you satisfied with the major emphasis of your life? If not, why?

2. Do you have an interest, talent, or hobby that you sense needs to be nurtured and developed in some way?

3. To what extent do you make connections between biblical principles and your actual work, not just your attitudes or relationships at work?

4. Can you see ways in which your work, work environment, workplace structures can become more shaped by your Christian values?

Helpful Resources

XI.
Resources for Marketplace Christians: Sampling and Evaluating the Materials

Scott Young

The previous decade has witnessed a tremendous surge in both the rhetoric and especially the activity of the ministry of the laity. One cannot ignore the increased emphasis on "marketplace ministry" or "the ministry of daily life." The mandate for this emphasis in the mission of the church is found in scripture and affirmed in the various traditions of the church.

Lay people's ministry in the world is undertaken with a sense of gratitude for the extravagance of God's generosity. God has given gifts to the people for their work and their play. These gifts become the resources that empower their daily ministry.

This ministry of daily life will be misguided as well as impotent if it is not directed and developed; direction is a theological task, development is a technological one. The theological task is to think critically and creatively about ministry. The technological task is to act confidently and competently. The essential interplay between these two—between knowing and doing—produces a ministry of the people that is both focused in its purpose and inventive in its operation.

All the people of God, including the *ordained* few who serve the many who are *commissioned* to work in the world, are required to struggle with the tensions inherent in the theological and technological tasks. We carry out our witnessing work in a provisional, complex, and ambiguous world. The routines of daily life that are connected with family, job, and community require both theological reflection and technological innovation. None of us, laity or clergy, can escape this responsibility as we live in the gap between our convictions and our responsibilities.

This is the framework for the resources that are available for the

ministry of the laity in daily life. Resources are the gifts and endow-
ments from God that enable us to do our work in the world. Resources
empower us to be co-creators with God as we shape and influence the
world. Resources also empower us to be embodiments of grace as we
evangelize and transform the world. Resources are indispensable to
fulfilling these two aspects of our Christian mission.

Corresponding to the recent upsurge in interest in the ministry of the
laity, there has been a proliferation of useful resources. My aim is to provide an assessment of some of these resources, emphasizing those that
deal with the workplace as a primary context of ministry. This sur-vey
will be limited to three categories—publications, institutions, and films.

General and Practical Publications

General Treatments

Marketplace Analysts

In the area of leadership in the workplace, we've seen best-selling
biographies of business celebrities (*Iacocca*), futuristic forecasting
(*Megatrends*), and calls for adventurous restructuring (*The New Realities*). The most widely recognized book is probably *In Search of Excellence*, by Peters and Waterman.[1] This influential work (not necessarily
the first or best) is largely responsible for elevating the "renewal at
work" theme into a larger, more public, discussion.

In this crowded arena, one book that stands out is Michael Maccoby's
most recent project.[2] *Why Work* is concerned with many of the same
topics found in the other books: productivity, renewal of corporate
cultures, effective leadership, and, as expected, prescriptions for future
success. But what makes Maccoby's treatment special is the depth and
sophistication he brings to every page. This is especially true of the way
he distinguishes between entrepreneurial and administrative leadership.
He argues that it is through the former that innovation and renewal will
occur. Also valuable is his exploration of the relationship between workers' values and their motivation and productivity. He demonstrates the
need for leaders to observe, understand, and negotiate with the values of
workers in order to help them reach higher levels of achievement.

Other key treatments of leadership include John Gardner's *On Leadership*, Burt Nanus' *The Leader's Edge: Seven Keys to Leadership in a Turbulent World*, and Steven A. Covey's *The 7 Habits of Highly Effective People*. Among these, James Autrey's *Love and Profit: The Art of Caring Leadership* deserves special attention. These books represent not only the latest ideas about leadership, but also deal with such vexing issues as: the dignity of the individual worker; loyalty to self, company, and society; values and motivational patterns; and productivity and quality of work. These authors are raising questions of a spiritual nature: calling and career choices, friendship and community in the workplace, and issues of meaning and lifestyle. These books also help us to understand the significant shift that has been taking place from a family-oriented to a job-centered culture.

A classic and dramatic record of people on the job is provided by journalist Studs Terkel's *Working: People Talk About What They Do All Day and How they Feel About What They Do.*[3] In interviews with a wide range of people, Terkel gains some perspective on how people understand their work, its meaning for them, and its effect upon their lives. In this prodigious collection, he captures the joy and sorrow, agony and ecstasy, passion and boredom, sacred and profane, both in the worker and in the workplace.

In *The Work of Nations: Preparing Ourselves for 21st Century Capitalism*, Robert Reich addresses the interrelationships of public policy, economic systems, and workplace productivity.[4] He guides us through the yet unfamiliar territory of economic and business realities that regularly trespass nation-state boundaries, including money, technology, and ideas. These relentless trends pressure corporations to acquire multinational identities and leave behind loyalty to a single political entity. He paints a stark portrait of the economic future for many of the world's workers. In addition to the familiar categories of manufacturing and service, he discusses a new category of business activity filled by symbolic analysts (workers who define problems and design solutions). This, he says, will be the group that makes economic gains in the future, but he raises serious questions about where such people will gain the core values, such as fairness and compassion, justice, generosity, and responsibility to do their work effectively. There are important issues and challenges here for people of faith.

Theological Assessments

There are a growing number of books in the area of the theology of the
laity and ministry in the workplace.

One of the most useful books for outlining a theology of the laity is
Richard Mouw's *Called to Holy Worldliness.*[5] In this lucidly written and
generally accessible work, Mouw first establishes the biblical notion of
vocation and then treats this as a manifesto for a liberated laity. This
book contains a passionate vision for the Christian who is willing to
respond to God's call for engagement in the world.

Another, more recent, contribution comes from Robert Benne, *Ordinary Saints: An Introduction to the Christian Life.*[6] Benne's purpose is
to demonstrate that ordinary people become saints not by heroic deed,
but in response to the faith, love, and hope that comes to them through
God's extraordinary grace. This helpful book connects the call of God to
the daily realities of family, work, public, and church life.

John C. Haughey offers us a fine book resource entitled *Converting
9 to 5: Spirituality of Daily Work.* The penetrating insight he offers into
a spirituality relevant to the workplace is hard to overstate. His theme is
that:

> The place of work is usually taken to be a worldly or secular kind of
> place to which God must be brought. A spirituality of work that
> thinks only in terms of bringing one's sense of God to work will
> inevitably become patronizing. If one learns to find God at work,
> one's spirituality will be nurtured and strengthened there . . . .[7]

A further Roman Catholic contribution to this area comes from
Rembert Weakland, Archbishop of Milwaukee. His book entitled *Faith
and the Human Enterprise: A Post-Vatican II Vision*[8] is a helpful interpretation of changes in the Catholic Church since Vatican II as they
relate to laity and their entanglement in the world. In a very helpful
section, Weakland charts recent developments in the engagement of
religion with public life. The most important aspect of this work is his
discussion on faith and money in which he outlines some of the most
pressing tensions for laity when the prevailing economic order produces
so much poverty. He carefully nuances the theological vision of the
Bishops' Pastoral letter *Economic Justice For All,*[9] and draws attention

to its inescapable implications for workers and workplaces. This book is refreshing in vision, thoughtful in style, and persuasive in argument.

Another highly recommended book comes from Miroslav Volf. His *Work in the Spirit: Toward a Theology of Work,* is a scholarly treatment of a neglected theological theme.[10] Volf is an Eastern European with significant experience with the West. His book covers a wide range of themes: meaning of work, analysis of economic systems, work and employment, work and transformation, dominant understandings of work, work and creation, and work and alienation. Of singular importance is Volf's contention that a theology of work emerges out of the dynamic of the Spirit. His view is quite different from the more static conception of vocation that has informed most Protestant thinking about work. The book pays careful attention to biblical materials, the complexities of modern societies, and the rigors of contemporary work, resisting all temptations to offer simplistic "how to" formulas.

A final theological recommendation is Douglas Meeks' *God the Economist: the Doctrine of God and Political Economy.*[11] In this provocative and challenging book, Meeks' chief contribution is to explore the relationship between the Trinitarian God and the expansive arena of economics. His discussions of such issues as scarcity, property, and human needs is stimulating and deserves sustained attention. Though it is a demanding volume, many marketplace and clergy persons would benefit from wrestling with it.

Practical Resources

Christian Practitioners

A number of important books on work have been written by active Christians involved in the marketplace.

The first is *Leadership is an Art* by Max DePree.[12] This book reads more like the seasoned wisdom of a saint than that of a CEO of a highly respected Fortune 500 Company. The author demonstrates clearly that sages can come out of board rooms as well as monasteries. The management enterprise, both in the corporation and in the church, can learn much from this manifesto on leadership.

I would also recommend *The Monday Connection: A Spirituality of*

Competence, Affirmation, and Support in the Workplace by William E. Diehl.[13] This very readable and engaging book serves as a catalyst for leadership in the workplace. Diehl draws illustrations from his world at Bethlehem Steel Corporation and illumines for us the challenges and opportunities for Christians in highly competitive situations. In a helpful manner he discusses themes that concern Christians in the workplace such as competence, power, status, servanthood, lifestyle, and compromise. Though not a book targeted specifically for management, his commentary would inform leaders at several levels who seek to be Christians on the job.

Lucid and anecdotal in style is *Secrets of People Who Love Their Work* by Janis Long Harris.[14] She portrays people who enjoy their jobs for a variety of reasons. The wide range of occupations and personalities that are presented yields a heart-warming exhibit of workers who have a strong faith-work connection. As well as showcasing enthusiastic workers, the author examines themes of money, mentoring, giftedness, balance, sacrificing, and finding God in our work.

There are several recently published resource materials that complement the more substantial works mentioned above. These practical treatments fall into four main categories:

Vocational Guides. The National Center for the Laity in Chicago has produced a series of booklets on the spirituality of work. The series currently includes issues on *Nurses, Teachers, Lawyers, Homemakers,* and *Business People*, and covers issues relating to Christian life at work, not just spirituality in the more technical sense.

Workplace Reports. A helpful report is *Faith and Work: Personal Needs and Congregational Responses*, from the Center for Ethics and Corporate Policy in Chicago. Also useful is Graham Tucker's *The Faith-Work Connection: A Practical Application of Christian Values in the Marketplace*. This includes reflections and value-analyses of the workplace developed by the King Bay Chaplaincy in Toronto, Canada.

Study Guides. Among the many guides for group study that merit attention are: *Christianity in the Workplace: Your Faith and Your Job* by Sean Eddington and Donald Orvis, part of the Lay Action Ministry Program series published by David C. Cook; *Behind the Scrim: Studies* *in Faith and Work* by Lee Taylor, from Christian Education Publications; *Getting the Job Done Right* by Robert Banks and Gordon Preece, published by Victor Books; *Satisfying Work: Christian Living from Nine to Five* by R. Paul Stevens and G. Schonberg, put out by Harold Shaw; and *Starting on Monday: Christian Living in the Workplace* by William Mahady and Christopher Carstens, published by Ballantine.

Audio Materials. Cassette tapes on different aspects of the work situation have been produced by a Catholic publishing firm and reflect certain denominational concerns. These tapes include J. Shea's *The Christian in the World* (Chicago: ACTA, 1988), J. Haughey's *Towards a Theology of Work* (Chicago: ACTA, 1989), and E. Marcianak's *A Worldly Vocation* (Chicago: ACTA, 1990).

Institutions and Periodicals

Christians seeking to reflect on their work life in a more formal and structured way can find quality resources at several institutions.

Graduate lay education opportunities are available at the following institutions. Regent College, in Vancouver B. C., was established as a graduate level school to provide theological education for laity at work in society as well as in the church. New College, in Berkeley, California has a similar mission. Both offer highly regarded winter and summer intensive courses as well as regular academic term programs. Other institutions, such as the Center for Christian Study in Charlottesville, Virginia; the Institute for Christian Studies in Austin, Texas; and Crossings in Louisville, Missouri, also offer theological training for laity.

Seminaries with specialized programs emphasizing "ministry in daily life" include Fuller Theological Seminary, Pasadena, California; Andover Newton Theological Seminary's Center for the Ministry of the Laity; and Auburn Theological Seminary, New York (primarily with workshops and seminars for congregations). The Center for the Ministry of the Laity also publishes a magazine focusing on the work of the laity in the marketplace. For a copy, write to the Center at 210 Herrick Road, Newton Center, MA 12159. These graduate theological graduate schools are ahead of the pack in developing a vision for theological education for the whole church.

Continuing education opportunities are numerous for those laity and clergy looking for formative stimulation and interaction. The Alban Institute offers a regular newsletter, a range of books—such as Verna Dozier's *The Calling of the Laity* and Davida Crabtree's *The Empowering Church*—and seminars around the country on the ministry of daily life. The Vesper Society provides a variety of resources, including a magazine, for equipping lay people in the marketplace. For a copy, write to the Society at 311 McArthur Boulevard, San Leandro, CA 94577. Marketplace Ministries leads workshops in colleges and congregations, has developed a manual for use in churches, and runs a widely aired radio program. You may contact them at P. O. Box 7895, Madison, WI 53707-7895. The Cathedral College of the Laity offers seminars, conferences, resource materials, and a newsletter; for information, write the South Tower, Washington National Cathedral, Mount Saint Alban, Washington, DC 20016. The National Center for the Laity is a volunteer group that provides seminars and conferences for the working Catholic, including occasional seminars and conferences as well as the "Initiatives" newsletter, a no-frills publication that is one of the best in the field. For more information, write the Center at 1 East Superior Street., #311, Chicago, IL 60611.

Substantial **marketplace magazines**, over and above those mentioned above, also deserve mention. *The Marketplace*, produced by Mennonite Economic Development Associates, deals with social implications of Christians in the marketplace and includes excellent critiques of works in print and available videos. It is available from MEDA, P.O. Box M, Akron, PA 17501. *Salt and Light* (formerly Executive Christian Woman) is full of informative articles, news, poetry, and other resources designed for Christian career women; it can be ordered from 1523 Silver Strand Circle, Palatine, IL 60074. *Ethics* covers a variety of issues in professional ethics, often focusing on a single major theme or workplace. The publication is sensitive to spiritual concerns rather than specifically Christian ones and is published by the Josephson Institute, 310 Washington Street, # 104P, Marina del Rey, CA 90202. *Business Ethics* is a secular publication with high quality, eminently practical articles, reports, and case studies. It is produced by Mavis Publications, Inc., 1107 Hazeltine Boulevard, #530, Chask, MN 55318.

A number of **denominational offices** are devoted to developing a variety of resources for congregations so that their members can deepen the faith-work connection. These ministry of daily life judicatories are not always widely known and are often underfunded. Despite these limitations, many of them do an excellent job in providing helpful materials. In addition to these nationally oriented organizations, there are a number of other organizations furthering laity's mission in the world. A recently formed group, the International Council of Leadership Foundations, sometimes called City Network, is a collection of urban-based leadership foundations that endeavor to involve the church in social problems in some of our large cities. The character and mission of these local organizations differ from city to city, but all seek to utilize congregational talent to solve some of the pressing urban problems. The most highly developed of these is the Pittsburgh Leadership Foundation that has now been in operation for fifteen years. The Foundation creates coalitions and partnerships between church, business, government, school, and community organizations to revitalize urban structures and renew declining neighborhoods.

Other **lay resource centers** exist at the purely local rather than national level in Chicago, San Diego, Spokane, and several other places. These centers make available seminars and materials related to work-related issues, recovery programs, community involvement, marriage enrichment, and theological education. Many of these centers were started to help meet a demand by individual Christians who wanted resources to empower their witness in daily life but could not find assistance in the church. These enterprises demonstrate a resurgent interest on the part of some laity to take their calling in the world with great seriousness. The emergence of local Centers for Ethics is yet another example of the rise of local attempts to connect faith and the workplace. The Center for Ethics and Corporate Policy in Chicago is one such organization that engages in research and programs that deal with values in the corporation. One helpful resource they have produced is the workbook *Faith and Work: Personal Needs and Congregational Responses*. Ethics Centers are springing up in other cities and are frequently connected with a church or related institution.

As with the survey of secular and religious publications, this over-view of institutions and periodicals is representative rather than compre-hensive. Many other organizations and magazines or newsletters exist to provide resources or services to lay people in the workplace.[15]

Films and Videos

We are living in a time when verbal and printed communication is being outpaced by visual communication, especially through the mass media. The spoken and written word will remain a powerful and necessary pre-sence. But the screen, both large and small, is the tool by which many of us gain interpretive as well as technical skill to understand our culture.

Various forms of popular culture—cinematic, theatrical, literary, musical—bombard us with ambiguous meanings and a diversity of va-lues, penetrating us with the pleasure and pain of our world and human existence. The arena of work is frequently portrayed in popular culture and gives us many clues as to how our fellow citizens view their daily life routines. These can provide helpful material for group discussion.

Films

First I would like to discuss some recent cinematic portrayals of work that can provide a stimulus for discussion of workplace concerns in a variety of teaching settings. Film is important because it vividly com-bines image and word drama and is accessible to a mass audience. Film, at its best, blends feelings and thoughts in a way that stalks the con-science. Movies prod us to view life from a new angle of vision. Cin-ema not only entertains but informs and changes us, enabling us to look at our workplaces and our job tasks in illuminating ways.

The following list is designed to give a glimpse of some recent and memorable portrayals of representative occupations and work situations: teaching: *Stand and Deliver* (1988) and *Dead Poets Society* (1989); journalism: *Absence of Malice* (1981) and *Year of Living Dangerously* (1983); military: *An Officer and a Gentleman* (1982) and *Platoon* (1986); law: *The Verdict* (1983) and *A Few Good Men* (1992); women at work: *Norma Rae* (1978) and *9-5* (1980).[16] With well dramatized, good stories that reveal the multiple dimensions of the workplace, these movies show the good, the bad, and the ugly aspects of working life.

I want to highlight three recent films that showcase job places and work related themes:

The first is *Do the Right Thing* (1989) by filmmaker Spike Lee. The plot is located in a Bedford Stuyversant pizzeria; the proprietor is a middle-aged Italian by the name of Sal. Mookie is the pizzeria delivery man. The major theme running through the film is tense race relations. One of the significant subthemes is work. *Do the Right Thing* includes (in addition to the pizzeria) a Korean fruit stand vendor, unemployed youth, and sports figures. Tom O'Brien commends the film:

> *Do the Right Thing* is not wildly revolutionary, as many sixties films were; in the figure of Sal, it celebrates hard work. Indeed, in its sympathy for white, blue-collar ethnics it is more generous than most recent movies made by whites on work-related subjects in our time . . . . [17]

Another film that deals explicitly with the workplace and the making of work is *Glengarry Glen Ross* (1992). This movie was originally a play by David Mamet and became one of the top movies of 1992.[18] It takes place in a real estate office and depicts desperate salesman (Al Pacino, Jack Lemmon, and Alec Baldwin) in a cutthroat competitive setting. The film explores the chaotic ways people struggle with meaning in their jobs in the context of dishonest co-workers, centralized corporate policy, performance demands, and declining market share. Themes of trust, loyalty, lying, strong-arming, manipulation, humor, success, and failure dominate this perceptive film.

The third film is Robert Altman's *The Player* (1992). This movie is a satiric treatment of the "blockbuster" atmosphere that currently pervades the Hollywood studios. The major character is a studio executive, Griffin Mill (Tom Robbins), whose primary responsibility is to listen to movie pitches in his search to find the next big hit. Griffin becomes the prototype of the 125-calls-a-day executive. He is emotionless and impeccably dressed, a consummate liar and compulsive careerist who has the reputation of championing script writers. The drama unfolds in a way that exemplifies the bottom-line strategy of big business and the harsh realities this imposes on people in a wide variety of jobs. The satire is pointed and has implications for most contemporary work situations. The humor in the satire reveals not an antibusiness bias but a moral demand for workplaces with values beneficial to individuals and society.

It is true, as Tom O'Brien comments, that:

Work isn't the strong point of many movies, for simple reasons. Most people don't go to films to see other people work; they go to escape their own. Moreover, if a movie does focus on one line of work, filmmakers risk offending its professionals who complain that their images were untruthful. To save time, costs, and research energy, and perhaps avoid complaints, filmmakers don't delve much into character's occupations. Characters are often given jobs to fill out their identities; less frequently are these jobs given real significance in the plot.[19]

Despite these limitations, films do convey important images and messages about daily life and work. Cinema does conjure up thoughts and emotions that sometimes lie buried in our souls. Filmmaker Paul Schrader states:

I think one is stung into progressive, positive behavior by an awareness of the great lure of negative thought . . . One of the things you should do in art is lift up the rock and look at those things inside you.[20]

Video Resources

Over the last few years several excellent videos relating to the workplace have been produced by religious organizations. Either in full, or through the use of excerpts, these can be valuable resources for either church-based or work-based groups. Among those that are available the following call for special mention:

Faith on a Tightrope is a two-part series featuring the ministry of the laity in their daily activities. Part I features an insightful commentary by Robert Bellah and Martin Marty. Part II offers a response to the issues and challenges raised by the first video. This series is available from the Cathedral College of the Laity, South Tower, Washington National Cathedral, Mount Saint Alban, Washington DC 20016.

Called to the Marketplace" is an ambitious four-part series enabling viewers to listen to marketplace Christians talking about their workplace challenges and opportunities. The series focuses on issues related to ethics, leadership, and evangelism. It is available from IVCF/Marketplace, 6400 Schroeder Road, P.O. Box 7895, Madison, WI, 53707-7895.

March 25—A Day in the Life of Catholic Laity in America portrays lay people working out their faith in diverse contexts including banking, social work, and the military. Of interest to Protestants as well, this video may be purchased through the Office of Publicity and Promotion Services, U. S. Catholic Conference, 1312 Massachusetts Avenue, N. W., Washington, DC 28005-4105.

Day by Day employs the film-within-a-film method to present a series of vignettes in which the actors explore the ministry of everyday life, one of which concerns an employee who is not working up to capacity. This is available from The Religious Film Corporation of America, P. O. Box 4029, Westlake Village, CA 91359.

Conclusion

This resource assessment concludes with a reminder that God gives good gifts to all His people to help direct and develop the ministry of the laity in daily life. The suggested resources are valuable tools for the theological and technological tasks the church must engage in as it witnesses to The Gospel and values of the kingdom of God in contemporary society.

Notes

1. Tom J. Peters and Robert H. Waterman, Jr., *In Search of Excellence: Lessons from America's Best Run Companies* (New York: Harper & Row, 1982).
2. Michael Maccoby, *Why Work: Leading the Next Generation* (New York: Simon and Schuster, 1988).
3. Studs Terkel, *Working: People Talk About What They Do All Day and How They Feel About What They Do* (New York: Pantheon, 1972).
4. Robert Reich, *The Work of Nations: Preparing Ourselves For 21st Century Capitalism* (New York: Knopf, 1991).

5. Richard Mouw, *Called to Holy Worldliness* (Philadelphia: Fortress, 1980).

6. Robert Benne, *Ordinary Saints: An Introduction to the Christian Life* (Philadelphia: Fortress, 1988).

7. John Haughey, *Converting 9-5: A Spirituality of Daily Work* (New York: Crossroad, 1989), 60.

8. Rembert Weakland, *Faith and the Human Enterprise: A Post-Vatican II Vision* (Maryknoll: Orbis, 1992).

9. National Conference of Catholic Bishops, *Economic Justice for All: Pastoral Letter on Catholic Social Teaching and the U.S. Economy* (Washington, DC: National Conference of Catholic Bishops, 1986).

10. Miroslav Volf, *Work in the Spirit: Toward a Theology of Work* (New York: Oxford University Press, 1991), 76.

11. Douglas Meeks, *God the Economist: The Doctrine of God and Political Economy* (Minneapolis: Fortress, 1989).

12. Max DePree, *Leadership is an Art* (New York: Doubleday, 1989), 92. His most recent book is *Leadership Jazz* (New York: Doubleday, 1992).

13. William Diehl, *The Monday Connection: A Spirituality of Competence, Affirmation and Support in the Workplace* (San Francisco: Harper Collins, 1991).

14. Janis Leny Harris, *Secrets of People Who Love Their Work* (Downers Grove: InterVarsity, 1992).

15. Information on Institutions identified here is available by writing to Marketplace Ministries, InterVarsity, P.O. Box 7895, Madison, WI 53707-7895 or by telephoning them at (608) 274-9001.

16. Tom O'Brien, *The Screening of America: Movies and Values from Rocky to Rain Man* (New York: Continuum, 1990).

17. O'Brien, 166.

18. Owen Gleiberman, "Movies: The Best and Worst 1992," *Entertainment Weekly* (December 25, 1992—January 7, 1993), 101.

19. O'Brien, 62.

20. Paul Schrader, *Schrader on Schrader and Other Writings* (Boston: Faber, 1990), 117.

Questions for Discussion

1. Is there any one idea, mentioned in the books covered in this survey, that resonates with your workplace experience?

2. Can you think of any other recent films or television programs you have seen that threw light upon the work environment today?

3. Which of the study materials listed sound as if they would be most helpful in a small group or Christian education program?

4. If you had to choose one work-related incident from which to develop a case study, what would it be?

XII.
Bringing the Workplace into the Worship Place: Celebration and Education for Worldly Ministry

William Diehl

In this book we have the opportunity to read how a manager, computer expert, media person, professional, teacher, builder, farmer, and homemaker each have been able to make the faith-work connection. These writers are to be congratulated and envied. Congratulated because they have discerned the faith-work connection and are able to articulate it; envied because they represent a minuscule part of the contemporary Christian Church that can make the faith-work connection.

Across our nation millions of devout Christians attend worship services every Sunday. Many of them also give long hours of volunteer service to their congregations by serving on committees, teaching in Sunday schools, and singing in choirs. Ask them how they serve God and they will invariably recite the various financial and time contributions they make to their church. Ask them if they serve God in their places of work, and they may be surprised by the question. Then, after some thought, they report that they follow the Golden Rule and don't lie or steal. That's it. Few indeed are the Christians who perceive the rich kind of faith-work connection presented in this book.

How can lay people be helped to see the ways in which God is at work in their occupational settings? Ideally, it would happen at the workplace. If it were possible in one's place of work to meet regularly with theologically sensitive lay persons or clergy, it is quite likely that one would soon gain a perception of the faith-work relationship.

Something approaching this was attained in programs once offered by the former Lutheran Church in America. "Connections: Faith and World" consisted of two major elements. In the first series of classroom sessions a trained clergy-lay team helped the participants to gain an understanding of God's universal presence in life. Explorations were

made of the worlds of family, occupation, government, and personal
relations. The Apostles Creed and the Ten Commandments plus numerous biblical references helped the participant to begin to make the faith-
life connection.

But that was all done in the classroom, at the church building.

The second part of the Connections program proved to be the most
exciting. It occurred in the participants' places of work. One by one,
each participant (there usually were about ten to twelve in a class) invited
the group to come to his or her place of work. Most often it had to be
after working hours. At times work could actually be going on. But in
each instance the host participant would explain in detail what he or she
did during a typical day of work. The group would then discuss how
they saw God's presence in this work. When I participated in the program several years ago, we visited a schoolroom, two factories, a medical supply outlet, a home, three business offices, a dentist's office, a
restaurant, and a department store. At the time, the workplace discussions did not seem particularly exciting, but upon reflection they were
dynamite. Now, many years later, we know what those workplace visits
really meant. We all now do better at making our "connections."

Unfortunately this highly helpful program fell by the wayside during
the formation of the Evangelical Lutheran Church in America.

Since it is difficult to bring the worship place into the workplace in
an effort to help people make their faith-life connections, how can the
workplace be brought into the worship place? How do we support members of our churches when we ask them to serve the institution?

Ministry in the Church

It is October and St. Paul's Church is about to launch its annual stewardship drive for next year's budget. Just before the sermon, Howard Rankin
goes to the front of the church and explains briefly why, as chairman of
the stewardship campaign, he is committed to giving time and money to
his Church.

Pastor Hines then follows with a sermon on stewardship in which he
praises Howard Rankin and all those other dedicated lay persons whom
Howard had recruited to give their time and energy to make home visits.
Following the sermon, those volunteers who have agreed to make stewardship calls are called up in front of the altar and commissioned by

Pastor Hines to "carry this Church's mission into the homes of all our people." Pastor Hines then asks the congregation to rise and asks, "Will you support and pray for these fellow members as they carry out their commission?" The congregations responds with a "Yes!"

On Tuesday night of the following week, a resource person from the diocese is present to train all of St. Paul's visitors in how to make effective stewardship calls. He uses a videotape and even leads the group through some role plays in which they all have some fun. Questions are invited and fears or concerns are addressed. The training session closes with coffee, fellowship, and a prayer of commitment. Just before the people leave, Pastor Hines announces that he and a few other stewardship veterans will be available "in case you have any questions or problems with which you need help. Just give us a call."

The stewardship visits are made the following Sunday and as the volunteer visitors return to the church to report on the pledge commitments they have received, they find Pastor Hines and Howard Rankin there to greet them and thank them for their wonderful work. Their results are posted on a blackboard as all eagerly await the final tally.

The following Sunday, Howard Rankin again gets up in front of the congregation to report the results of the stewardship drive. He then asks all the volunteer visitors to rise while the congregation gives them a big round of applause. Following the service, the visitors and their families are treated to a very nice "thank you" lunch in the fellowship hall.

That scenario, or variations of it, is played out in thousands of American churches every year, as hundreds of thousands of church members carry out their lay ministry to their church. These same people then go into their weekday world but with little sense of having a Christian ministry there.

Can congregations use the model that has been proved so successful in having lay persons do ministry in the *church* to help them with their ministries in the *workplace*? I think so.

Equipping for Ministry in the Workplace

Let's imagine, if you will, that St. Paul's Church made a major commitment to affirm, equip, and support all their laity for ministry in the world. Since there are so many arenas for the worldly ministry, let's suppose they decided to concentrate initially on the field of public education.

Pastor Hines contacted Rebecca Quinto, a Junior High School principal, to see if she would agree to be the leader for the program. She agreed. Rebecca's first step was to go through the congregation's directory to make up a list of all those whose work is in any way connected with the field of public education. It was an easy job because St. Paul's lists the names, addresses, phone numbers, and occupations of everyone in the congregation. Her church defines *occupation* as that which occupies most of one's time. Paid jobs and unpaid jobs are occupations. For retirees, the directory lists their primary pastime or volunteer work. For children, their grade in school is listed.

Rebecca collected a list of about twenty-five persons: five teachers, one school superintendent, two school bus drivers, two school nurses, two school board directors, one custodian, two cafeteria workers, three volunteer teacher aides, one counselor, three administrative clerks, and so on. A letter went out to each of them, signed both by Rebecca and Pastor Hines, asking them to participate in a six-month program designed to connect their faith with their work. Out of the twenty-five, all but three agreed to participate. They were asked to be sure to attend the Church service on a certain Sunday. The Sunday was billed as "Ministry in Education Sunday."

The special Sunday came and, just before the sermon, Rebecca Quinto stood up in the front of the church and talked about why, as chair of this project, she is committed to living out her faith in her job in public education.

Pastor Hines then followed with a sermon in which he affirmed the ministry of Christians in education. He also praised Rebecca and all those other dedicated lay persons whom Rebecca had recruited to participate in the project on Ministry in the Public School.

Following the sermon, the twenty-two public school workers were called up to the altar and commissioned by Pastor Hines to "be the ministers of this church in the field of public education." Pastor Hines then asked the congregation to rise and asked them, "Will you support and pray for these fellow members as they carry out their commissioned ministries in our public education system?" The congregation responded with a "Yes!"

In short, within the worship service, a ministry to the world was affirmed before the congregation just as strongly as a ministry of stewardship within the congregation.

On Tuesday night of the following week, and on every Tuesday night for six months, Rebecca met with the twenty-two people to help them to become more intentional and effective in their Christian ministries in the workplace. Because of the constitutional separation of church and state, it was clear from the start that no overt witnessing to their faith could be part of their strategy. Instead they talked about creative, redemptive, providential, justice, and compassionate dimensions of their work. From time to time, Rebecca brought in a consultant to help with an especially thorny problem. Bible study and prayer became a routine part of their study periods. They used videos and had fun with role playing. Pastor Hines dropped in from time to time to listen and learn but he made it clear that they, not he, were the ones God had called for ministry in their public schools.

In short, the same type of support, educational resources, and commitment used for training for in-house lay ministry was used for training for worldly ministry.

As the months passed, the Tuesday night group became extremely supportive of each other. Furthermore, there was a built-in accountability to the support group. When one person shared a problem with the group and suggestions were made for possible strategies, that person wanted to keep the group updated on his or her progress with the strategy.

At the end of the six months' period, a second "Ministry in Education Sunday" was held during a worship service. This time Rebecca Quinto preached the sermon and told the congregation of the many ways the group was able to become more sensitive to and skillful in ministry in their places of work. She asked the group to stand and the congregation applauded. Pastor Hines stood up and spoke of how impressed he was with what the group had done.

The six-month period had ended but a funny thing happened. During that time the group had become so close and had become so deeply aware of their ministries in the field of public education that they decided to keep on meeting monthly. The group still is a place for its members to go with concerns, it still offers help, and it still is a place where Christians are accountable for their ministries in the workplace.

A month after the "Ministry in Education" group got started, a second group was formed for people working in public service. It followed the same steps as the first group. A month after that, a "Ministry in Business" group got started. Then came "Ministry in Homemaking." There was "Ministry in Retirement" and "Ministry in the Classroom" for high school students. On they came, one new group each month, until everyone in the congregation had the opportunity to be affirmed, equipped, and supported for their ministries in daily life.

Then a strange thing happened. St. Paul's stopped having annual stewardship drives. Once the members began to connect faith and daily life, their worship life became more important, and their support of their Church, both financially and in volunteer service, grew.

Howard Rankin joined the "Ministry in Industry" group because, as the CEO of a small but fast growing company, he saw multitudes of opportunities for Christian ministry.

There were small occupationally-related groups meeting all over the place. All the groups were led by lay persons. Pastor Hines' role was to be a biblical or theological resource person, when needed, and to constantly affirm all that was going on.

In my present congregation we have tried most of the elements of this approach for bringing the workplace into the worship place; we have not yet pulled it all together. We have tried some other things, however.

The Monday Connection

One of the most successful ways of connecting worship and work has been our Monday Connection group.

The Monday Connection is a group of people from The Lutheran Church of the Holy Spirit in Emmaus, Pennsylvania. They meet for breakfast at 7:00 a.m. the first Monday of each month at a local restaurant to discuss the everyday implications of being a Christian.

At each session one of the members has prepared a personal, real-life case study, and copies are distributed to all participants. We also ask each presenter to be especially attentive at the prior Sunday's worship service to see ways in which the worship speaks to the case study he or she is presenting.

Group members arrive at the restaurant promptly at 7:00 a.m. One offers a prayer and then food orders are taken. While the food is being prepared, there is always good socializing. By twenty minutes after seven we are finished eating and copies of the case study are distributed.

After they have been read, the questions begin. "What do you mean by __?" "Can you give me more detail on __?" "How do you feel about __?" Once the group has clarified the issue, members think of options. "Have you ever thought about __?" "What would happen if __?" Frequently these options are hotly debated among the group. We often find that one of the group has faced a similar situation and is eager to share that experience. We never tell someone what to do. We provide options and debate them. That, in itself, has been of great help to the one presenting the case study.

Our pastor and director of lay ministries usually attend as biblical or theological resource people. From time to time one of them will call for time out while a biblical or theological connection can be made.

We are out promptly at 8:00 a.m. so that people can get to their jobs. At the close of each session, we ask if someone will volunteer for the next month's case study. No one is pressured to present a case study, but someone always seems to come forth. The case studies tend to relate to problems or decisions that must be faced at the person's place of employment. But not always. Several cases have related to family problems. The fifty case studies we have dealt with over the past five years have been varied and challenging.

One manager told of an employee who was assigned to a lonely location where his job was to insure the safety of a transmission station. There was reason to suspect that the employee was sleeping on the job. The only way to find out was to spy on him. Should the manager authorize surveillance of the employee to insure safety, or should the employee be trusted? Which is the greater Christian responsibility, to customers or to the individual?

Another case involved an elected County Commissioner whose closest associate on the Commission was constantly grandstanding before the press to gain name recognition for future elections. Nothing illegal was ever done, but sometimes the actions bordered on being unethical. The group member pointed out, however, that she received support from the self-aggrandizing Commissioner on important issues and frequently they stood alone on issues that were politically unpopular.

She asked the Monday Connection group if she should distance herself from a person whose tactics she did not support at the risk of losing an important ally.

A plant manager who had experienced many painful years of dealing with a son who was on drugs told of how some of his employees came to him for help with their children. However, the union contract at the plant required that a union representative always be present when management met with an employee. The only way to have effective and confidential drug counseling with the employees who sought him out was to keep it secret from the union. Should he risk trouble with the union and his own corporate management for violating this part of the union contract?

One person spoke about dealing with a very sexist boss. Another asked about what to say to an aged person who wanted to die. Someone else talked about a brother who was constantly taking advantage of a mentally retarded sister.

All of these instances point to the same question: What would Christ have me do in this situation? Our pastor has stated repeatedly that the case studies have been very helpful to him in understanding the kinds of issues parishioners face.

Whenever possible, the group tries to find ways in which the worship service of the previous day connected to the case study being presented. Was there something in the lessons, the sermon, the liturgy, or a hymn that related to the problem? More often than not we have found no connection; this was a sobering discovery for our pastor. While we recognize that a worship service cannot possibly relate directly to the specific needs of 250 different people, we have learned to look harder for connections to our everyday lives. And our pastor has become more intentional about faith-life connections in his sermons and prayers.

The group was started by lay persons and is fully maintained by lay persons. The pastor and director of lay ministries are not responsible for any part of the program, although they have, on occasion, presented their own case studies. Their primary contribution to the process is to be on-the-spot theologians.

The Monday Connection runs from September through June. This enables people to drop out at the end of a cycle instead of going on forever.

Each August our church sends a letter to about forty persons who might have an interest in being a part of the next cycle of the Monday Connection. The letter explains the purpose of the group and indicates that the next cycle of meetings will run from September through June of the following year. A return postcard is enclosed to indicate if the person wants to be put on our mailing list for the forthcoming cycle. Usually about half of the people contacted respond favorably to the invitation. They go on the mailing list.

About ten days before the first Monday of the month, postcard reminders from a lay leader go to all names on the mailing list, indicating who will be presenting the case study. Participants are asked to respond by phone, indicating whether or not they will attend, so that the proper number of reservations can be made at the restaurant. If no word is received by the Friday prior to the breakfast, a member follows up with a phone call. We believe the postcard reminders with phone follow-up are key factors in maintaining a high attendance pattern.

For many people, the Monday Connection has supplied the only means for them to discuss some of the vexing issues of life with a group of committed Christians. The normal routine of congregational life provides few such opportunities. In fact, a few of the regulars have indicated that the Monday Connection has been one of the most meaningful experiences they have ever encountered in their church life. One new member of our congregation said, "This has been the most exciting thing I have experienced in any church to which we belonged."

Adult Education

The adult education program of a congregation is an obvious forum for helping people make the connections between their faith and their daily lives. Unfortunately, there are very few denominational materials available that deal with workplace issues. There are some, but once a class uses them, what next?

Some churches successfully develop study programs by using some of the better faith/work books that have come out in the past few years. The article on resources for churches and groups in this book provides some excellent leads for such purposes.

The Center for Faith and Life

Our congregation is large enough and has enough talent that we can develop our own courses. A few years ago we scrapped our entire adult education program and formed our Center for Faith and Life. Since we see our people's ministries occurring in four primary arenas—Occupation, Family, Community, and Church—we decided to set up each one as an individual learning track. In addition, a fifth learning track, which we call Foundational, offers basic biblical and theological courses as well as introductory courses to Ministry in Daily Life. On any given Sunday three of the five tracks offer programs for members of our congregation. The Foundational track runs every Sunday; the other four tracks alternate, running a month at a time. The Foundational track is usually taught by the pastor; all other programs of the Center are lay designed and lay led. The Ministry in Occupation sector deals with a broad range of issues our people face in their occupations. Some programs are very general and span all occupations; others are specific. Some of the general topics offered have been: Managing Disagreement; Giving and Receiving Criticism; Biblical Perspectives on Honesty in Business; Affirmative Action; The Christian as Supervisor; Security, Loyalty, and Obsolescence; The Changing Work Force; Creative Interviewing; How to Move Again; Successful Performance Appraisals; Empowering Employees. Topics that focused on more specific occupations were: A Business-Education Partnership; Christians With Public Responsibility (a judge, an elected county official, and the publisher of our newspaper); Science and Technology (Are we "playing God" in Genetic Therapy, Medical Technology, and Micro Electronics?); and Issues in Education.

In these courses we probe biblical and theological connections and, at times, that can be hard going. The Center for Faith and Life has been a huge success. In terms of numbers, it has more than tripled our adult education participation. But in terms of relevance and helping people to make the Sunday-Monday connection, it has been outstanding. The complaint we like most to hear is "There are so many good things being offered at the same time that I don't know which one to attend."

Other Suggestions

Some congregations have a practice of devoting a specific Sunday worship to ministry in one's occupation. Frequently, people are asked to come to church dressed as they will be at work. The pastor focuses his or her sermon strictly on ministry in occupation.

Some congregations will have a Sunday in which, during the offering period in the worship service, people are asked to come to the altar with symbols of their work. Such things as tools, computers, stethoscopes, chalk, date books, and heavy gloves are placed on a large table before the altar as symbols of our offering of work. (Everyone gets their symbols back, of course.)

We have done both the work clothes and tools' approach in our congregation from time to time. They are only symbolic, however. While they affirm ministry in one's work, they do not get into the issues of the workplace and how our faith connects with them.

The key to bringing the workplace into the worship place is the pastor. If he or she has to have tight control over everything, it will not happen. There are two reasons why the pastor should not totally try to control: Very few pastors have the breadth of knowledge of workplace issues to be able to design educational programs of relevance. Secondly, lay leadership must be involved in both the planning and presentation of programs in order to give them credibility in the eyes of the rest of the congregation. The pastor must be willing to let people experiment with ways to bring the workplace into the worship place. The pastor's role then becomes one of affirming and supporting the efforts of the members of the congregation, providing them with good biblical and theological help, and insuring that the congregational worship experiences will nurture and inspire the people.

Our experience has been that prayer, experimentation, and trust in the workings of the Spirit are leading us toward a richer connection between the place of worship and the place of work.

Questions for Discussion

1. How much does the workplace feature in the prayers, songs, sermons, and commissionings in the weekly corporate worship in your church?

2. To what extent is the adult education program in your church helping to prepare people for their ministries in the workplace?

3. Which elements of the vision for equipping the laity in this article would be most difficult to incorporate or could most easily be started in your church? Why?

4. What would have to be done to begin a Monday Connection group in your congregation?

XIII.
TheThreefold Call:
The Trinitarian Character
of Our Everyday Vocations

Gordon Preece

> . . . the great social and cultural maladies of the modern age all have
> this one common characteristic: that they deny personal vocation. . .
>
> Denis de Rougement[1]

Introduction

My purpose in this chapter is to relate vocation and the trinitarian God. I
will explore God's nature as a divine dialogue or trialogue in which each
person—Father, Son, and Spirit—calls the others to fulfill their varied
vocations in the story of creation and the *economy*[2] of salvation. Use of
the term economy is deliberate, for this eternal economy and the earthly
one we spend our working lives in overlap. God's threefold calling over-
flows into our lives, calling us to bring the paraphernalia of our everyday, economic lives into the life of the Trinity just as God enters eagerly
into our everyday existence and working life, "pitching a tent" among us
(compare Jn. 1:14), and making a home in our world.

From Calling to Career

Our call is more than our work, particularly "paid work," and it also
means something other than a "career." The word career comes from the
same root as our word "car." It means to travel, usually by oneself.
Career is an individualistic concept.[3] Spouse, children, church, political,
and environmental responsibility are all meant to give way to the person

careering along the freeway of success. A recent report on higher education shows that "the careerism of the American undergraduate rules out all but a cursory effort at cultural knowledge . . . . Students are simply preoccupied with what they think will help them get a job—at the expense, sadly, of what helps us have a culture."[4]

By contrast, "a calling, as opposed to a career, implies a belief in the intrinsic value of a given line of work."[5] It isn't a mere means to an unrelated end, as a career is to success. Instead a calling is for the sheer joy of it.

A calling is also for others as much as for its own sake. Vocation was originally focused on the common good. The early English Puritans distinguished between the general calling of all Christians (to be Christian, to walk worthy of one's calling, to belong to the church, to journey toward the kingdom of God) and each individual's particular callings (singleness or family, work, and citizenship). If there is a clash between our general and our particular callings, then the general calling has priority.

Around the mid-seventeenth century, Puritanism became more individualistic and dualistic, and this was carried to America's shores. Separation between sacred and secular developed in the greater priority given to Sunday worship. General and particular callings drifted apart. Calling came to equal occupation. With the separation of economics as a technical science from the moral sciences in the eighteenth century, calling gave way to calculation, vocation to career. Economics and work increasingly become a law unto themselves. The idea that "business is business" came into being.

While the vocabulary of vocation was still on people's lips, it increasingly gave only a religious veneer to the *status quo*. Eventually we ended up with that embarrassing (now deleted) verse of the Victorian hymn *All Things Bright and Beautiful*, "The rich in his castle, the poor at the gate, God made them both, and ordered their estate." Each was to stay in their calling.

This misuse of vocation to maintain an obedient and submissive work force was aided by the advent of deism. This viewed God as the once intricate designer but now remote observer of the world. God was no longer intimately involved in creation's workings. It was more like a machine, not a living work of art in which the artist is involved. As a result, things largely go their own way, controlled by rigid natural laws (significantly the founder of modern science, Sir Isaac Newton, was a deist and nontrinitarian). This view of God set the scene for the mechanistic and depersonalizing effects of the Industrial Revolution, scarring both the environment and our collective psyches.

Newton's utterly unchangeable natural laws became the paradigm for the social order as well. An immutable order of callings kept people in their places and identified them by their social roles, often losing sight of their full humanity. As a Scottish gravestone allegedly says: "Here lies the body of Thomas Jones, born a man, died a grocer . . . ."

Alienation and Vocation

Much of the church went along with this natural and social model for fear of the sort of disorderliness seen in the French Revolution. The long-term effect was to alienate large bodies of workers and to abandon the creative sense of work or vocation to the Romantic writers (who exalted work as art and craft) and to the Marxists (who exalted work as the essence of humanity).

According to Marx, just as our human essence has been alienated and projected upon an imaginary God, so our creativity had been objectified into products that were taken away from us by the owners of capital for mere monetary gain. This was no better than "wage slavery."

By contrast, vocation is part and parcel of being a person with a sense of purpose or calling.[6] Even before we are born, we are called into being as persons by the expectations of significant others. As they address us and we respond, we discover our sense of time and place, the context of our calling, and slowly form our identity or self. That is why names (standing for identity) are often changed at the time of one's call in Scripture—Abram becomes Abraham, Saul becomes Paul. We are, or become, what we are called.

To summarize then, "The identity of a person is formed or deformed through the calls of others and God . . . ."[7] Through creation we are called into dialogue with God, but in the Fall this responsiveness was short-circuited. But we have been re-created through the call of Christ, who like God makes the deaf hear and makes all things whole (Mk. 7:37). He is the place where God's call and our response meet.

In this way vocation provides the basis for developing a distinctively

Christian critique of alienation, for alienation not only infringes the two-way conversational character of those made in God's image, but violates our nature as persons with a sense of God-given purpose. Treating people and products as mere means denies the end we were created for—to glorify and enjoy God forever.

Alienation not only effects people's work, but can have catastrophic feedback effects on their faith. Exodus 6:9 describes how the Hebrew slaves' oppressive work made them unable to answer God's call to liberation.[8] A young man reflects on the same experience today: "In college my fragile faith bit the dust. Working at a truck line loading freight crushed the vision of Camelot."[9] Persistent alienating experiences in the workplace can alienate us from God.

If the problem of alienation was partly brought on by a deistic notion of God, then a key aspect of the solution is a rediscovery of the Trinity and the Incarnation. In the early nineteenth century, the Romantic poet Samuel Coleridge saw human creativity as an echo or incarnation of God's eternal creativity. The Christian socialist and theologian F. D. Maurice also stressed that the Father should not be viewed as a hard taskmaster arbitrarily demanding atonement by the Son, thus alienating the members of the Trinity from one another, but rather as acting together with and in Christ. On this trinitarian and incarnational basis of divine community, Maurice developed a sense of national and working community in industrial England.

Trinity and Vocation in Conversation

These alternatives point the way to setting vocation in the context of a dynamic, trinitarian view of God. A helpful image here is that of God as worker,[10] who created the world using two hands—the Word and the Spirit. Unfortunately, many Christian traditions are in their own way one-handed, amputating or failing to use their other limb. We need to become ambidextrous again.

All Christians are tempted by various forms of unitarian (or one-dimensional, nontrinitarian) theology. We tend to focus on a favorite member of the Trinity to the neglect of others.[11] To learn from their strengths and weaknesses, we will look at three different Protestant traditions which, though trinitarian, have each emphasized one member of the Trinity more than the others.

Vocation and Creation

Lutherans (and Calvinists) have traditionally anchored vocation by an
unbreakable chain to God as Creator. When distorted by a static, deistic
view of creation, this has led to such abuses as among the patriotic
German Christians in the 1930s, who simply obeyed the law and did
their jobs without asking any questions about Jewish genocide. Today it
can also lead to an unchangeable view of vocation which, like ordination,
is lifelong, and therefore ill-adapted to modern mobile work situations.

Sadly, Luther's use of "Law" had conservative connotations that
were later misused to endorse the *status quo*, with little room for the
spontaneity of creation. While a sound reaction against confusing church
and state, separating law and government too much from Gospel and
conscience allowed great scope for the world of politics and work to
become a law unto themselves, commandeering vocation. The Gospel
was increasingly confined in later Protestantism to providing forgiveness
for a guilty conscience rather than forging a new world. The Gospel
afforded comfort in a compromised world rather than confronting and
healing the whole person and the whole of life.

Today efforts are being made to recover Luther's original vision of
God's creative involvement in human vocation.[12] Luther emphasized
God's continual creativity, sustaining life against the forces that would
wilt and destroy it. From our birth to our death, God is constantly creating, bringing new life and fertility out of barrenness.

The major area where God is constantly innovating is in our vocations. They are vehicles for God's vitality. Through our everyday
domestic, workplace, and political roles God is at work creating, nurturing, and maintaining life. The woman who works to provide for her
family is doing this no less than the woman with her child at her breast.
Both are, in Luther's terms, "masks" of God through which the majestic
God, who Moses could not bear to see, is represented through our daily
tasks as we play our particular part in the divine drama.

For Luther, the neighbor we meet and serve through our vocations is
truly a wondrous reality, literally reeking of God. It is here that law and
gospel, everyday demand and eternal forgiveness, intersect. Dying and
rising with Christ is played out in a kind of daily passion play in the
parents who postpone some of their own interests for their child, or the
teacher who stays behind after a hard day to help a struggling student.

To Luther's mind the law meant mobility and change as our neighbor's needs were met through our vocations in ever new and creative ways. In fact, the tools we work with are vehicles of God's Word—constant reminders to serve our neighbor in our work.

Vocation and Christ

In the nineteen twenties and thirties a Reformed reaction arose against the German Christian overemphasis on "law" and "order."[13] This new view also shied away from an emphasis on God the Creator and stressed the role of the second person of the Trinity. This resulted in a more dynamic understanding of vocation that responded to one's freedom in Christ through the Gospel. Unfortunately Calvin's original emphasis on the pre-existent Word as the mediator of creation, as well as of salvation, was muted. This meant that our primary vocation was to be involved in Christ's reconciling work, bearing witness to Christ by proclamation and service.[14] This is a view that many Christians hold.

This view recognizes, however, that in order to witness to Christ, we have to provide for ourselves, by working to meet our own and others' needs. We work to live, not live to work. This is the raw reality of work that does not need to be varnished over by identifying vocation with making a great cultural contribution. As the playwright Bertholdt Brecht said, "First comes grub, morality afterwards!"[15] Though work is necessary, it is peripheral to God's central work of reconciliation. It is only a part of "the active life" Christians are called to lead, a part that is subordinate to prayer, witness, and service.

Work is not, however, worthless or inhuman. In Christ, the truly human one, we find criteria for truly human work, work which is an analogy to the personal relationship between Father and Son in the Trinity. According to these criteria, work should:

1. draw people to give their best with heart and soul;
2. express human rationality, allowing time to think;
3. develop community in the workplace, not isolation;
4. value, affirm, develop, and enhance human existence; and,
5. allow for leisure, reflecting the biblical priority of Sabbath over work.[16]

These criteria, while not exhaustive, are certainly suggestive. They
ask the right questions—that a new work ethic must answer questions—
especially for those most severely affected by the current employment
ethic: the unemployed (often including the sick and disabled), the bored
worker, and the workaholic.

This Christ-centered perspective gives vocation a dynamic sense of
freedom and transformation, rather than anchoring it to a static social
order. However, this freedom is not arbitrary, but is defined and focused
through Christ and the prominent lines of God's providence in our lives.
All the limiting (but in God's providence liberating) factors of age, cir-
cumstance, history, and aptitude involved in each person taking up his or
her special responsibility or calling are encompassed by it. This allows
for greater flexibility in work, more fluidity between home and workplace, more provision for self and others, rather than professionalism. In
this way we reflect a greater range of God's creativity.

Vocation is not restricted just to our job, and so does not exclude
children, the sick, the elderly, unemployed, and homemakers. Even
those who have a profession do not exhaust their vocation in their job but
imitate God's action in a wide array of different spheres. Rather than
imprisoning us in a particular position or social order for life, it is a
moment-by-moment process of being open to God's providential com-
panionship. What abides is the call, not the sphere of service.[17] This is a
liberating word for all those who don't find their calling confined to
conventional notions of employment.

Still, this Christ-centered view never completely succeeds in over-
coming the marginal place it assigns to creation. The nature and range of
God's creativity are reduced to a mere backdrop or stage scenery for the
chief character in the divine drama, Christ.[18]

Vocation in the Spirit

While vocation has traditionally been located in relation to God as
Creator, and in the twentieth century to Christ as reconciler, it has only
recently been related to the Holy Spirit.[19] The rediscovery of Calvin's
cosmic understanding of the Spirit and modern Pentecostal perspectives
provide new resources for correcting an overly creation-centered view of
vocation. Creation takes place in the Spirit. The Spirit is "the fountain

of life," poured out on all things. The Spirit breathes through the whole living fabric of creation, setting the scene for people venturing to work (Ps. 104:30,23). Through the Spirit, creation speaks of God and is also sustained, not statically (as traditionally assumed), but waiting in suspense to reach its goal and destiny of the "new heavens and new earth" (Rom. 8:22ff). In this way, the Spirit is the dynamic link between original creation, providence (or continuing creation), and new creation.

Instead of a nostalgic longing "to get ourselves back to the garden,"[20] this portrays creation not as a "closed system," but as a system open to change. Continual creation involves, not just as for Luther a personal encounter with our neighbor, but nature itself.

The worker does not merely impose order on a reluctant, inert matter, but "in a sort of dialogue with her material . . . lovingly coaxes it into revealing its potential." God's Spirit is present in the nonhuman creation that is the object of work and prompts its longing for liberation. The same Spirit gives inspiration and guidance to working people who "cooperate with it, mindful of its longing to participate in the glorious liberty of the children of God (Rom. 8:21)."[21]

Rather than the threefold traditional orders of labor, family, and state in which one's vocation was played out, this view speaks of "ordering processes"[22] that point to the end or goal of creation keeping institutions and areas of life open to it.[23] Human conditions then become more mobile, changeable, and movable than before. Only God's kingdom is unchangeable. This fits well with the more dynamic, mobile character of modern work and social roles.

In the midst of the modern separation between the real-self (found in romance, leisure, therapy, and spirituality) and the role-self (found in work, politics, family commitments), our identity and integration does not come from some isolated sense of self, but through God's call to mission and hope. Social callings are then judged not by their capacity for self-realization, but by the possibilities they offer for incarnating or fleshing out our faith. The criterion for choice and change of calling then becomes: Does it point in the direction of the kingdom?

This Spirit-centered and future-oriented perspective warns us against putting all our eggs in any earthly vocational basket,[24] rightly emphasizing the Spirit's involvement in the world, not some separate sphere of spirituality. But it also requires correction. It overemphasizes the Christian call to resist assimilation to society and be a constant source

of positive unrest and change (the Exodus and Exile aspects our calling).
These, however, clearly presuppose creation as a source of stability and
as the ground of resistance and transformation.[25] As Jesus showed us,
drawing out God's original "purpose" in creation (Mt. 19:4-8, Mk. 10:4-
8) sometimes demonstrates just how radical a creation orientation can be.
To be really radical means getting to the created root of things. The
images of the future drawn from creation, such as we find in Revelation,
also spell out what the freedom of the end will look like.

Vocation Between Creation and New Creation, Between Father, Son, and Spirit

So Christian vocation needs to be rooted in the created structures of this
world, but ready to be uprooted at a moment's notice to move towards
the new creation. We are always on call for the kingdom, living in the
creative tension between the varied vocations of the members of the
Trinity in terms of creation and recreation. We are called to be
Abrahamic, Exodus people, constantly on the move toward the kingdom
and promised land. But we are also called to rest with David (2 Sam.7)
and put down deep roots in land, family, work, city, even exile (Jer. 29:3-
9). Jesus not only called His disciples *away* from their jobs to answer
His call, but He also regularly called those He healed to take their healing back home with them, to *stay* where they were called (Mk. 5:18ff,
5:34, 8:26; Mt. 8:13, 9:6).

The Master not only said to "hate" (not give first loyalty) to families
before God (Mk. 4:31-35), but He also told the Pharisees not to leave
aged parents without support in the name of a higher calling (Mk. 7:9-
13). Paul not only advised people to "stay in the calling in which you
were called" (1 Cor. 7:20, 17, 24) but because "the appointed time has
grown short; from now on, let even those who have wives be as though
they had none, and those who mourn as though they were not mourning,
and those who rejoice as though they were not rejoicing, and those who
buy as though they had no possessions, and those who deal with the
world as though they had no dealings with it. For the present form of
this world is passing away."

Both dimensions of Christian vocation are important. Which one
should be emphasized at any particular time is a matter for spiritual and

corporate discernment. The mark of true wisdom and prophecy is its timeliness. But in a time dominated by change for change's sake, when loyalty in family, company, and community seems to be forgotten and rootlessness has reached epidemic proportions, there is a place for a renewed emphasis on the orders of creation, for staying in one's calling. Thus, if it involves a rightful place for the reconciling work of Christ and remains open to the call of the Spirit, it may not be a conservative stance but a rare form of radicalism. In the end, the issue is not whether we start with Father, Son, or Spirit, but where we end. Do we encompass the whole narrative of Scripture—the story of creation, salvation, and re-creation—and so provide a full and dynamic context for our view of vocation? If so we find reason to sing with the fisherfolk "God has called us, He will not fail us. God has called us, we will not fail Him."

Notes

1. Denis de Rougement, *The Christian Opportunity* (New York: Holt, Rinehart and Winston, 1963), 37.

2. Economy is made up of two Greek words, *oikos* (house) and *nomos* (law), and simply means the rules of the house or household management, from which it got its expanded modern technical meaning.

3. William May, "Career, Calling, Profession," (unpublished paper, Southern Methodist University, 1988), 6.

4. L. A. Times 11/1/92 editorial referring to Clifford Adelman, *Tourists in Our Own Land: Cultural Literacies and the College Curriculum* (U. S. Department of Education, 1992).

5. Christopher Lasch, *The True and Only Heaven: Progress and Its Critics* (New York: Norton and Co., 1991), 522.

6. Alistair McFadyen, *The Call to Personhood: A Christian Theory of the Individual in Social Relationships* (Cambridge: Cambridge University Press, 1990), 9.

7. Op. cit., 116-120.

8. Miroslav Volf, *Work in the Spirit* (New York: Oxford University Press, 1991), 166.

9. Quoted in Diogenes Allen, *Traces of God* (New York: Cowley, 1981), 1.

10. This, and the image of God as worker, are borrowed from the second century Church Father Irenaeus.

11. See Richard Mouw, *The God Who Commands* (Notre Dame: University of Notre Dame Press, 1990), Chapter 8, and H. Richard Niebuhr, "The Doctrine of the Trinity and the Unity of the Church," *Theology Today* 3 (October 1946), 371-384.

12. Gustaf Wingren, a Swedish Lutheran theologian from a working class background, is the major representative of this view. See his *Luther on Vocation* (Philadelphia: Muhlenberg, 1957).

13. This was spearheaded by twentieth century theologian, Karl Barth, who was a pastor in a Swiss industrial village before teaching theology full-time. He was involved in worker education, unionism, and socialism.

14. Karl Barth, *Church Dogmatics*, IV/3, trans. G. W. Bromiley (Edinburgh: T.& T.Clark, 1961), Ch.16, Sec.71 where "vocation" is treated under the doctrine of reconciliation.

15. Quoted in David Meakin, *Man and Work: Literature and Culture in Industrial Society* (London: Methuen, 1976), 6.

16. Karl Barth, *Church Dogmatics*, III/4, 470-574.

17. Op. cit. 595ff.

18. Barth loved the music of Mozart, but rarely, if ever, refers to the sheer grandeur of the Swiss Alps.

19. Jurgen Moltmann is the primary representative of this perspective, though his student Miroslav Volf has followed it through more thoroughly in relation to work (preferring the concept of gifts to that of vocation). See further his trilogy *God in Creation, The Way of Jesus Christ,* and *The Spirit of Life* (all published by Fortress Press).

20. Popularized in Crosby, Stills, and Nash's 1970's anthem *Woodstock.*

21. Miroslav Volf, *Work in the Spirit* (New York: Oxford University Press, 1991), 146 quoting N. Wolterstorff, "Evangelicalism and the Arts," *Christian Scholar's Review,* 17 (1988), 466.

22. J. Moltmann, *The Church in the Power of the Spirit: A Contribution to Messianic Ecclesiology,* trans. M. Kohl (New York: Harper & Row, 1974), 164.

23. J. Moltmann, *Hope and Planning,* trans. M. Clarkson (London: SCM Press, 1971), 118, 105. These processes are economic, political, and cultural.

24. J. Moltmann, *Theology of Hope: On the Ground and Implications of a Christian Eschatology,* trans. J. W. Leitch (San Francisco: Harper Collins, 1991 [1967]), 329-334.

25. Terrence E. Fretheim, "The Plagues as Ecological Signs of Historical Disaster," *Journal of Biblical Literature,* vol.110, No.3, (Fall 1991, 385-396 and "The Reclamation of Creation: Redemption and Law in Exodus," *Interpretation,* (October 1991), 355-356.

Questions for Discussion

1. On which member of the Trinity do you most focus in your faith and approach to work?

2. In what ways could each member of the Trinity enrich your concept of vocation?

3. Ask yourself the following questions about your work? Is it done properly and wholeheartedly? Is it worthwhile or good work? Is it done cooperatively or in isolation and competition? Is the work of inner self discipline or reflection encouraged? Is your work limited or seemingly limitless?

4. How does the tension between creation and new creation affect your different vocational commitments (in the broader sense of family, work, citizenship)? How can Christians help each other live with these tensions?

XIV.
The Faith-Work Journey:
Developing and Deepening the Connection
between Faith and Work

Janet Hagberg

How did you choose your career? Was it a family legacy? Did it grow out of strong interests or talents you exhibited as a teenager or college student? Or is it a mystery to you how you ended up in the field you're in?

No matter how we chose our careers, whether they are paid or volunteer, we all can engage in meaningful and productive work activities. And no matter what our work is, we can find a way to relate it to our faith journey. Even before we are conscious of our faith we live it out in our work anyway, in the way we treat other people and in the ways we seek meaning in our vocation.

I propose that we will gain more satisfaction in both our faith and our work if we are more conscious of and attentive to the connection between them. And if we probe the interrelationship diligently, we will find deeper connections than we ever realized between faith and work.

For so many of us the two are separate, distinct parts of our lives. But if we view them together, faith and work can be part of an organic whole. And if we understand and cultivate the connections between the two, life changes can result.

To explore the connection between faith and work, I offer two premises. First, where we are on our faith journey determines how we behave at work, what our motives are, and how we live out our vocational call.

Second, we can strengthen the connection between faith and work by consciously applying the skills and talents we use at work to promote our spiritual growth. More on that later. Let me start with the first premise.

I am suggesting that where we are on our faith journey affects how we behave and how we live out our calling as God's people in the world. To that end, I will describe six stages in the life of faith as they influence the world of work. The stages are summarized from *The Critical Journey,* co-authored by the late Rev. Dr. Robert Guelich and myself. The six stages are:

Stage One:　The Recognition of God
Stage Two:　The Life of Discipleship
Stage Three: The Productive Life
Stage Four:　The Journey Inward
　　　　　　The Wall
Stage Five:　The Journey Outward
Stage Six:　The Life of Love

In describing faith as a journey, we could use faith as a noun, adjective, or a verb. If we use it as a noun, we would ask "do you have faith?" meaning a set of beliefs and practices. As an adjective, we ask, "what faith are you?" meaning, which particular set of beliefs do you practice? As a verb, we describe faith as a dynamic process that changes as we grow. For this model, faith is a verb, an active process encouraging us to let God be God in our lives.

The word journey suggests an image of travel with no instant goal, perhaps meandering, stopping along the way, learning as we go. In my experience, and in listening to others' journey stories, this is an apt description of the journey of faith.

Although we move through the stages in order, these stages are fluid and cumulative, with each stage building on the previous stages, like an ever-widening upward spiral. We may pass through many different stages in the course of a day or in different parts of our lives, but we have a *home* stage where we currently feel most comfortable. It is possible to get stuck at any stage and stay there indefinitely.

I will discuss each stage by describing it briefly and giving an example of the connection a person living in this stage of faith has with his or her work, along with the advantages and disadvantages the stage offers. Remember, you can recycle to any of the stages over and over again, and you can be in more than one stage at the same time.

Stage One: The Recognition of God

At this stage, faith is recognizing God. We are becoming aware of a higher power in our lives. Some of us entered the spiritual journey for the first time as children, others as adults. Some of us can name where and when this happened, others just know it happened. We enter this stage either from a sense of awe or a sense of need. We are awed by God's glory, which we perceive in the miracles of nature, birth, healing, music, or love. If we enter this stage out of need, it is the result of pain, rejection, or guilt from which we seek release. Many people experience this stage at mid-life when they discover a quest for greater meaning in life or long for a new purpose.

Work Connection: There seems to be little obvious connection between faith and work at Stage One. Sometimes that lack of connection is what brings people to God. We focus most of our energy on our relationship with God whether that means experiencing awe, recognizing our deep need, or accepting our powerlessness. What we do spiritually at work is largely unconscious. We may even take a spiritual hiatus from work by separating our spirituality and our work, in order to concentrate on our faith.

For example, John, a senior executive in a corporation, found himself at age forty-six flat on his back in intensive care with a heart attack. He'd been very successful in the family furniture business yet here he lay connected to machines that sustained his life. He began to wonder what use his career had been if it ended up endangering his life. And he admitted to himself that he never really wanted to be in the family furniture business in the first place. Along the way he'd been too busy to engage much with his kids, except on an infrequent vacation. He decided he needed to review his life, part of which was to connect with his dormant spirituality. There he might find meaning. But he wasn't sure how.

Advantages of This Stage: We need our energy for total concentration on ourselves and our relationship with the Holy. Faith needs to be uncomplicated at this stage and there is little possibility for a strong or conscious faith work connection.

Disadvantages: We are self-absorbed and can feel disconnected from our work entirely. We need to guard against self-pity or martyrdom, lest we miss the meaning of this stage as an invitation to growth.

Stage Two: The Life of Discipleship

At this stage, faith is learning about God. We apprentice ourselves to others now, taking in everything we can to grow in faith. Our meaning comes from belonging to groups of like-minded people who teach us about our spirituality. We seek answers from our leader or a cause, feeling secure and right about our faith. We are excited and energetic, eager to engage with others and to keep learning.

Work Connection: We want a *concrete* connection between our work and our faith. We want to learn and then share our faith by serving God within the church, the community, and at work. We strive to study, build our skills, and get support from others. Our exact faith-work connection differs whether we come from conservative, mainline, or liberal traditions. Examples are working on justice issues at work, striving to use our work talents wisely, witnessing to others about our faith, striving to be ethical, focusing on prayer and meditation, working in a church-related organization, finding our right niche, or attending meetings of spiritual co-workers.

Jane is an example of this stage. She is a nurse in a retirement and nursing center. She heard her pastor say we need to speak of our faith to others at work. When one of the women residents suddenly became ill and wept uncontrollably, Jane asked her if she wanted to pray. The woman nodded and Jane prayed a simple prayer for her. The prayer calmed the woman so they could attend to her health needs.

Another example is Mike, an accountant. He feels his greatest witness of his spirituality is to be a competent and truthful professional, treating each client with care and respect. His daily morning discipline of quiet time assists him to have a calmer day and to view more clearly the needs of his clients.

Advantages of This Stage: Our needs are well served by the faith community through personal growth programs, Bible study, support groups, Twelve-Step groups, prayer, classes. We are ready and eager to learn, as faithful and loyal members of our community.

Disadvantages: We are vulnerable to strong leaders and can be misled. Sometimes we are so clear about the rightness of our approach, we think others who approach faith differently are wrong. And our zeal can inadvertently offend others.

Stage Three: The Productive Life

At this stage, faith is working for God. We have arrived. We feel special to our community now that we're finding our niche. Responsibility and leadership roles interest us as ways to use our gifts and talents. We value the symbols of the spiritually fruitful life, whether those be the gifts of the spirit, respect, recognition, or reaching spiritual goals. We want to teach others how to live out their faith as we have learned.

Work Connection: We have found the concrete connection between skill, competence, and faith. We practice our faith regularly through church, causes, evangelism, or in the work world. Our competence and confidence are high so we can move to new levels of responsibility or to new arenas, like advanced study or acting as a mentor for others. We are in the position to teach others what we have experienced about faith and work.

Conscious of ourselves as role models, we monitor our work decisions, practices, and treatment of others. Our management and leadership styles represent our faith values. We believe what we are doing represents God's will in our lives and we strive to do it as competently as we can. Success is one measure of our faithfulness.

Susan is a good example. She is a professor of management at a local college. She feels it is not only her responsibility but also her ministry to teach ethical practices to her students. She also teaches ethics at her church as a volunteer and works at a food bank occasionally on weekends. She is very satisfied that she found ways to connect her faith and her work.

Ezell is an elected county commissioner. His faith is reflected in his commitment to poor and neglected people in society. He also works with young African American teens to help them improve their self-worth and job skills. Occasionally he meets with other elected officials of faith for mutual support and encouragement.

Sandra is a homemaker who has watched her children and their friends struggle with the teenage doldrums. She and some other mothers started a Teen Review at their church. It is a talent show in which teens find out what they do best and display their talent in the show. Talents include computer programming, dancing, singing, cartooning, stitchery, sports, writing, gardening, dress design, etc. You name it, and it becomes a new addition to the Review.

Advantages of This Stage: We use our best skills and competence in working for God. Freedom of choice allows us to operate our lives on our firm faith principles. We feel energized and successful.

Disadvantages: It is easy to become too busy or weary in well doing, thus eroding our faith. Mistaking success for faith can feed our egos. Hypocritical behavior can damage us and others. Excesses of this stage can cause arrogance, even abuse.

Stage Four: The Journey Inward

At this stage, faith is rediscovering God. This stage represents a major turning point in our faith. As a result of either a faith or life crisis, or a long flat plateau, we begin questioning and doubting what previously was clear and defined. We question the behavior or intention of a previous leader or practice. Confused, we begin an inner search for direction and meaning. Along the way we may become disenchanted, even drop out for a while. We pursue personal honesty and integrity with God, letting God out of the box, renewing our image of God.

Work Connection: At this stage our work frequently feels meaningless. We think work is the issue, when it is just the symptom of a faith or life crisis. WE are the issue, not work or God. We were running the show. Now we need inner transformation; we must live into the struggles we are having with faith, God, life. We may fear, hate, or disregard work, yet we long for purpose. We spend a great deal of time wondering how our values and our work can ever be connected. We feel inconsistent, without direction. Yet somehow we continue to work. And through all this we are already being transformed personally. In our own vulnerability, we are better listeners, more compassionate, better mentors, more able to exhibit fairness. We are separating ourselves from the compulsion to "do" something. We are more able to "be."

Jamie had been a youth group director in a national Christian organization and burned out from repeated, disguised sexual harassment from her boss. She couldn't bear to talk about it because she feared no one would listen. And it affected her faith, casting doubt on her sense of call to this ministry. She decided to drop out and consult with other youth organizations for a year while she tried to find where God was in this whole mess. Questioning whether she was even Christian any more, she sought spiritual direction to sort out her feelings and her faith.

Hal always thought if you were competent and did the right Christian things, life would work out. That was before he lost his job in a corporate restructure. He got depressed and remained unemployed for a year, questioning why his faith wasn't working. A pastoral counselor talked with him about God having other things for him to experience during this time. Hal got more interested. Maybe God was still part of this after all, but in a different way.

Advantages of This Stage: We can use our limited energy to concentrate on our relationship with God, and slowly give up what we were worshipping—work, money, family, talents, success, leadership. We have immense compassion and connection with other searchers. We are open to a new way of living.

Disadvantages: We are self-absorbed and appear selfish and unavailable to others. Seeing no spiritual connection to work, we could get stuck in the searching and "crazy" with the confusion.

The WALL

The Wall is that mysterious place where our will meets God's will face-to-face. It is an excruciatingly wonderful part of the faith journey. We approach The Wall, kick it, remove one stone, and put it back again. We decide to come back again later, much later. Or we pick out one or two stones and examine them. What emerges for us are all the things about us that The Wall hides; our woundedness, our hidden addictions, our shadows, our childhood pains, our self-absorption.

We may even feel totally abandoned by God for a time. But slowly we begin to *see*, to *feel* the pain in our core, to be *embraced* by the loving grace of God in a new way. We experience The Wall through self-reflection, tough love, prayer, keeping a journal, therapy, and spiritual direction. The personal quality most necessary in facing The Wall is courage.

Work Connection: As with Stage Four, the Wall suggests more of a connection with self and God, less consciously with work. Yet transformation is already happening. Personal and work transformation requires that WE get out of the way. At The Wall we are deeply aware of our woundedness and are willing to let God heal us. We are merely trudging in our life of faith; yet we can identify with all the other trudgers around us. We are in a community of people who know what their core is; and out of our core will come our new calling. We can see glimpses of a more calm and serene place. There is hope at The Wall.

Lucinda is a physically disabled woman who for years had been a successful consultant. But she had a series of devastating business partnerships with well-meaning but chemically addicted men. She struggled with her faith throughout those business experiences because she thought God had abandoned her. A special retreat weekend with a gifted counselor helped her realize she grew up in an alcoholic family and because of her background she was drawn toward "dangerous people." She began the slow healing process. And she brought God back into the process. God had gotten mixed up with the family system as a bad guy, but now God needed a different role. Her pain brought God out of the box and allowed God to be both feminine and masculine, loving and strong.

Advantages of This Stage: We know we are "getting" it, letting God be God in a new and transforming way. We find meaning in and through the pain. Inside, we are doing God's work, which leads to transformed work on the outside. This is our time of gathering wisdom for a different role of leadership in the world.

Disadvantages: We are God-absorbed, feeling our pain and woundedness acutely, misunderstood, rarely connected emotionally to work, often disconnected from others. We are in The Wall.

Stages Five and Six:
The Journey Outward, The Life of Love

At this stage, faith is surrendering to, and reflecting, God. Our life's meaning comes from discerning God's purpose for us. We embrace our brokenness as the basis for our spiritual calling. Out of a calm, grounded place, we focus on our passion, even to the point of giving up important things or people in our lives. Pain allows us wisdom and new freedom without having to suffer. We live in obedience to God, with Christ as a model of compassion.

Work Connection: Our crucial work is prayer, discernment, self-care, listening, obedience, wholeness. Out of those practices our *real* work in the world emerges, no matter what work we do for a living. Our focus changes.

We gravitate slowly and personally to the toughest issues of the world that are largely "unsolvable," like love, peace, poverty, violence, homelessness, bigotry, economic inequality, abuse, disease. Our role is not primarily to solve the problems, but to be a powerful presence in the midst of the unsolvable situation and to work in our own way in easing pain. Success is not as important as faithfulness.

Our best work comes out of our weaknesses: then we are dependent on God. We are servant leaders. God does things through us we never knew we were capable of, using skills we didn't know we had. Our spiritual egos diminish so we can practice tough love and take risks others might consider unthinkable. And our creativity, in whatever form, soars. It doesn't matter what our occupation is as long as we can live out our calling through it.

Esperanza learned from many painful and racist experiences in her life that God is always there in the middle of it. Her counseling experience taught her about the inner courage needed to name the abuse and do something to free herself. Now she knows the most important gifts are peace and clarity even in the middle of chaos. In her outer work she owns a housing development company, but her real work is loving and working in her Hispanic community. She works as an advocate for the women because at her core she understands their pain. The biblical story of Queen Esther is her model, a woman who risked herself to save her people. Esperanza risks herself by speaking out against abuse and taking in teenage girls who have run away from abusive homes. She is teaching her niece to run the business so she can be about her "work" with fewer interruptions.

Jeff is a high school coach in an inner city school. As a child, his father abandoned him. In his thirties, he revisited the pain of that loss and worked with an elder of great faith in his church to find a new, loving, father relationship with God. Now, as head coach he works with individual kids on their school work, relationships, and parental issues. He thinks of himself as the adopted father to many of the boys on the team. And they come back to see him for years after they graduate. He lets his assistants manage the mechanics of training and running plays. A few years ago he made a pledge to find a person in the community to put the kid with the highest grades on each senior team through college. So far five successful men have sponsored athletes.

Advantages of This Stage: We experience freedom from choices. There is no burnout, no anxiety, no fear of fear itself. We do not inflict our pain on others. Hearing God's daily direction, we need not be in charge. If asked, we can risk our lives.

Disadvantages: We appear impractical, foolish, illogical. Frequently we do not make the best use of our skills and talents by other's standards. We are not successful in the usual ways of measuring success.

Now that I have shown that the connection between faith and work falls in neat categories, I will reiterate that faith is a journey, fluid and flexible, meandering, mysterious, and unpredictable. We move back and forth and all around. We can even be in more than one stage at a time, in different parts of our lives. For me, the most important insights of this stage model are an understanding of and an appreciation for where I am on the faith journey, and an appreciation of where others are who are different from me.

Using Work Skills to Develop Our Faith

All these examples have shown how our faith journey affects, transforms, and nourishes our work. But what about the other way around, using our work skills and talents to develop or nurture our faith? By applying our work skills, be they creativity, discipline, critical thinking, or nurturing to our faith we contribute more consciously to deepening of our faith. By way of illustration I will give brief examples of those four work-related skills applied to spiritual practices.

Let's say you do creative things at work; designing, writing, composing, landscaping, or drawing. I am suggesting you apply these skills in your spirituality. Draw your faith journey experiences, write in a journal, compose poems of your life experience, design new ways to talk to God. Pen your favorite spiritual quotes in calligraphy.

Maybe you have a discipline, whether educational, business, or managerial. You can apply your discipline of research, organization, planning, time management, risk taking, and evaluation to your faith journey. Take a risk in your faith or spend time every day on a spiritual practice and observe the changes in your life. Give yourself a performance appraisal on your faith work connection. Write your faith covenant with God, including your own mission statement.

Let's say critical thinking and analyses are important to your work. Study a portion of scripture in depth to learn about it's historical and cultural significance. Take classes that will encourage you to ask the questions that help you make sense of your faith. Write a position paper on a issue of faith that is important to you.

Perhaps nurturing is a large part of your work in child care, health professions, or counseling. Apply those listening and empathetic skills to your faith. Listen for God. Develop intimacy with the Holy. Set up a self-care program for yourself. Be empathetic with your own spiritual wounds and compassionate with people of other faiths.

Sometimes it is helpful to approach our spirituality with a practice that is not as familiar to us. It takes us to a new part of ourselves and we can break through barriers more easily. So, if you are familiar with analyzing, try sitting in front of a burning candle and feeling the presence of God. If you are adept at nurturing, try writing or speaking out on what you are experiencing.

To reiterate, the connection between faith and work is two-way, making the two a unified whole, like the Yin Yang symbol in Asia. Our faith journey informs our behavior and values at work, and our work talents and skills can develop, enliven, or deepen our spirituality.

One sure way to grow spiritually is to ask God to deepen the way in which we think about our faith and work connection. Deepening our faith is what the Critical Journey is all about. But we must be careful what we ask for. We might get it.

Questions for Discussion

1. What is the most important way in which you live out your faith in your work?

2. Which stage of faith do you identify with most in your life now?

3. Have you found a way to consciously nurture or develop your spirituality? How?

4. What issues did this article raise for you?

BIOGRAPHIES

Julia Banks

Julia Banks has combined a commitment to homemaking and gardening
with a range of other activities. She has been involved in the planting,
developing, and networking of house churches in Australia and North
America. She is keenly interested in spirituality and journal keeping, and
is a sought-after workshop leader among lay people, seminarians, and
pastors. She has written a number of articles in this area, helped produce
curriculum resources, and, with her husband, co-authored a book entitled
The Church Comes Home: A New Basis for Community and Mission.
Currently she is living and coordinating a community house with theological students in Pasadena.

Robert Banks

After spending time in pastoral and academic work in Australia, Robert
Banks became a theological consultant to various occupational groups
and grassroots Christian communities. He was also a Fellow of an
Institute for Church and Society in Canberra. He has edited and written a
number of books on the connection between faith and everyday life, the
most recent of which are *Redeeming the Routines: Bringing Theology to
Life* (Victor), and *God the Worker: Journeys Into The Heart, Mind and
Imagination of God* (Judson). He is currently Homer L. Goddard Profes-
sor of the Ministry of the Laity and Chair of the Ministry Division at
Fuller Theological Seminary.

Richard Begbie

Coming from a long and distinguished line of clergy, after time in secular and pastoral work, Richard Begbie heeded the call of the land. He lives and works with his wife Carla and three children on a family farm in the hills near Canberra, the Australian national capital. This has been the base for a number of creative environmental initiatives. Many of his tales and reflections appear in *The Canberra Times,* to which he contributes regularly. His children's story, *Tennant's Gold,* was recently published by Brolga Press.

Perry Bigelow

Born in Michigan and raised in Florida, Perry Bigelow has been a home builder in the Chicago area for over twenty-five years. He is probably best known for building affordable homes and for his housing and economic development initiatives in the inner city. He is a member of various Boards of Directors and Advisory Councils including the National Association of Home Builders, Energy Efficient Building Association, and Illinois Department of Energy, as well as the Chicagoland Prison Fellowship, MidAmerica Leadership Foundation, and InterVarsity Christian Fellowship's Marketplace. He is also an Adjunct Professor at the Eastern College Graduate School of Business.

William Diehl

For most of his adult life, Bill Diehl has had one foot planted solidly in the world of business and the other in the world of the church. He is president of a management consulting company and has served on the boards of directors of several steel companies. He previously was a Manager for Sales of the Bethlehem Steel Corporation. He is on the National Council of the Evangelical Lutheran Church in America, is President of the Lutheran Academy, and has served in various capacities with a vari-ety of organizations dealing with the ministry of the laity. In his efforts to help people connect faith and daily life, he has taught, spoken, and written extensively. His most recent book is *The Monday Connection* (Harper).

Donald E. Flow

Don Flow is President of the Flow Automotive Companies, operating Chevrolet, Buick, Saturn, Ford, Lexus, Honda, Acura, BMW, Volkswagen, Porsche, Audi, and Hyundai dealerships. He is an Elder at the First Presbyterian Church. Married with three children, he serves on a number of civic, organization, and educational boards. As he puts it, he has "attempted to think about my calling infusing each sphere of life (church, family work, political, and civic)."

Steve Garber

Steve Garber is on the faculty of the American Studies Program, an interdisciplinary semester of study in Washington, DC, sponsored by the Christian College Coalition. He has been teaching for fifteen years in a variety of settings, including continuing commitments to InterVarsity Christian Fellowship, the Coalition for Christian Outreach, and the C. S. Lewis Institute. He and his wife Meg both serve on the board of Rivendell School, where three of their five children are students.

Janet Hagberg

Janet Hagberg has been active in her own business of consulting, writing, and speaking for seventeen years. She has written four books, *The Inven-turers* (with Richard Leider), *Real Power*, *The Critical Journey* (with Robert Guelich), and *The Silent Witness Story* (with Carrie Bardwell). She is a certified spiritual director and a licensed social worker. Her first love is volunteer work with women in prison and her passion is working to reduce domestic violence. Janet is a member of Colonial Church (UCC) in Minneapolis. She is married and has two sons in college.

Sandra Herron

Sandra Herron is currently Vice President and Manager of Sales and Service Development at NBD Bank in Indianapolis, Indiana. She holds a

business degree from Indiana University and an MA in Theology from
Fuller Theological Seminary. She also serves on advisory boards for
Inter-Varsity Marketplace, Fuller Theological Seminary, United Way,
and the Salvation Army. Sandra considers the marketplace her "mission
field" and is a frequent speaker on issues related to the integration of
Christian faith and work.

Hal Miller

After completing doctoral work at Boston College, Hal Miller taught
philosophy for ten years, first at Stonehill College, then at Worcester
Polytechnic, and finally at Northeastern University. He was then recruited by a high-tech firm, TASC, that was looking for someone to do
process improvement for them so they could see the "big" picture. He is
now writing metasoftware (software that writes software) and has been
happy ever since. He has written a book on the abortion debate and has
served as one of the editors of *Voices in the Wilderness* magazine. He
can be reached by e-mail at hmiller2tasc.com or on Prodigy where his ID
is VXGJ40A. He is married with two children and lives in Salem,
Massachusetts.

Mary Munford

Mary Munford lives in Redondo Beach, California. She works in Los
Angeles as a television news writer. She is a graduate of UCLA, California State University Northridge, where she studied political science and
journalism, and Fuller Theological Seminary where she completed a
Master of Arts in Theology. She is involved in a Media Group exploring
the connections between faith and work. Mary has received several
Emmy Award nominations for her feature reports on religion and society.

Gordon Preece

Australian born Gordon Preece's vocations include being married to
Susan and father of three spirited children. He has also been a youth

worker, associate and senior pastor, and regular adjunct professor at a local seminary. He has written widely in magazines, journals, and books on the areas of work, ethics, and Christian lifestyle. He is completing doctoral work at Fuller Theological Seminary in the theology and ethics of vocation and is committed to developing and empowering lay ministry. Currently he is Academic Dean and Lecturer in Church History at Ridley College, an Anglican seminary in Melbourne, Australia.

Edward A. White

Ed White undertook his theological education at Union Theological Seminary in New York and McCormick Theological Seminary in Chicago. Initially he was pastor of Good Shepherd-Faith Presbyterian Church and later became Associate and then General Presbyter of the National Capital Presbytery. Over the last few years he has been involved in teaching, networking, leading workshops, and conducting research on laity issues. Currently he is a Senior Consultant at The Alban Institute.

Scott Young

After completing a Master of Divinity degree at Denver Theological Seminary, Scott Young was involved for some years in campus ministry. Presently he is the director of Marketplace Ministries West for Inter-Varsity. He created a course on Media Ethics for the Film Studies Center in Los Angeles and, as adjunct faculty at Fuller Theological Seminary, co-teaches a course on Values in the Workplace. He and his wife Kathy live with their three children in Long Beach, California.